ultimate
dog groomir

ultimate
dog grooming

Eileen Geeson
Additional material by Barbara Vetter & Lia Whitmore

FIREFLY BOOKS

A FIREFLY BOOK

Published by Firefly Books Ltd. 2004

First Printing

Publisher Cataloging-in-Publication Data (U.S.)

Geeson, Eileen.
    Ultimate dog grooming / Eileen Geeson ; additional material by Barbara Vetter & Lia Whitmore. —1st ed.
[288] p. : col. ill., photos. ;   cm.
Includes index.
Summary: Step-by-step guide to grooming all major dog coat types, and on starting a dog grooming business.
ISBN 1-55297-873-7
1. Dogs -- Grooming. 2. Dog grooming industry. I. Vetter, Barbara. II. Whitmore, Lia. III. Title.
636.7/0833 21   SF427.5.G44 2004

National Library of Canada Cataloguing in Publication

Geeson, Eileen
    Ultimate dog grooming / Eileen Geeson ; additional material by Barbara Vetter & Lia Whitmore.
Includes index.
ISBN 1-55297-873-7
    1. Dogs--Grooming. I. Vetter, Barbara II. Whitmore, Lia III. Title.
SF427.5.G43 2004   636.7'0833   C2003-905182-X

Published in the United States in 2004 by
Firefly Books (U.S.) Inc.
P.O. Box 1338, Ellicott Station
Buffalo, New York 14205

Published in Canada in 2004 by
Firefly Books Ltd.
3680 Victoria Park Avenue
Toronto, Ontario, M2H 3K1

Printed and bound in Hong Kong, China

Author Eileen Geeson with her dogs.

DEDICATION

This is dedicated to Jeanne Beady, who gave me my first grooming job. I thank her for her kindness to dogs and for her expert, caring knowledge. Also to Gigi, the first Poodle I clipped.

ACKNOWLEDGMENTS

Special thanks to Carol and Mandy at DeZynaDog for their help and encouragement, and for allowing me to use their salon and up-to-the minute equipment and products in the preparation of the dogs profiled. Thanks to the dogs and their owners who patiently sat through hours of grooming and photography, namely Pippa Clare, Barbara Thornley, Martin Butler, Kevin Dodds, Ron Ellery, Leslie Curry, Molly Jones and Cathy Browne.

I thank the following for their help with the breed profiles: Val Watkins of Valsett (English Setter), Carol Ritchie (Griffon), Linda Mayne (Spinone Italiano), Terry Spencer (Welsh Terrier), Gael Stenton and Ann Kemp (Lagotto Romagnolo), Gael Stenton (Spinone Italiano diagrams and additional information), Violet Slade (Black Russian Terrier), Jan Wakerley (Irish Water Spaniel) and Marita Bott of Bardonhill (Irish Setter). Many thanks to all the breed clubs and advisors who checked or gave advice on their breed profiles. If you would like further information on a breed, or its grooming requirements, contact the relevant breed club (your national kennel club will have details). Photography: Sally Anne Thompson and R. Willbie. Line drawings: Viv Rainsbury.

Contents

grooming methods (clipping; hand-stripping; rolling; carding; thinning); general checks and procedure (anal glands; nails; dewclaws; ears; eyes; teeth); time per groom

PART THREE: BREED PROFILES

1 COAT TYPES

Many people think grooming is all about clipping Poodles, but it is much more than that. Grooming is the act of keeping the skin and coat in a healthy, clean, balanced state. It also involves the maintenance of teeth, ears and nails.

Grooming is an integral part of dog care. Not only does it keep the animal clean and looking good, but it is also a social act that strengthens the relationship between handler and dog.

How you groom a dog depends on the breed, coat type and the owner's personal preferences. Anyone can put a dog on a table and brush its coat up and down for a few moments, but with a little thought and hard work, both dog and owner can enjoy the experience and, who knows, you may be a future Groomer of the Year as a result!

BUYING A DOG: COAT CONSIDERATIONS

Among the many breeds of dog, there is a tremendous difference in the types of coat. Certainly, one should take this into serious consideration before taking on a breed of dog.

- Can you cope with the hair?
- Will the dog require professional grooming help? (See Chapter Four.)
- Can you afford the outlay of regular trips to the grooming parlor?
- Are you, or any of your family, asthmatic or allergic to shedding dog hair or dandruff, or both?
- Could you cope with all those long curls that get covered with mud during a wet walk?

You may be attracted to a breed with a luxurious coat (left), but can you cope with the reality of keeping it clean and well groomed?

These are just a few questions that need to be considered before deciding on the right breed for your family. It is wise to speak to owners of your shortlisted breeds before making your final choice.

Your national kennel club will be able to put you in contact with breed clubs of those types of dogs you might be interested in. The club representatives can tell you how demanding the coat care is for their particular breed so you will know exactly what you will be taking on.

It is a good idea to consult a groomer to inquire about the cost of grooming sessions before making a final decision on which breed is right for your family. Additionally, groomers, who have worked with dogs of many breeds for many years, often have valuable knowledge to impart about the characteristics of different breeds.

For full information on grooming different coat types and the equipment needed, see Part Three.

PUPPY COATS

Puppies of all breeds have a softer coat than they will have on gaining maturity, and it is easy to underestimate the grooming that is required as the dog matures.

Poodles, for instance, have a soft, fluffy wool coat that is easy to keep until they are about 7 months of age, when the coat will thicken. Unless it is properly groomed, the coat will mat or felt against the skin, especially if the coat gets wet and is left to its own devices to dry.

The Bearded Collie coat is quite manageable at the puppy stage (left) but the adult below requires regular attention.

You are what you eat – a glossy, healthy coat is proof of good nutrition.

The raw, meaty bones diet is popular with many owners.

vegetables and, two or three days a week, a meal made from brown rice and chicken is a healthy, natural diet for a dog.

Additives are not generally required with this diet, but some dogs may benefit from evening primrose oil, flaxseed oil or starflower oil, at a dose of 500 mg daily. This is especially beneficial when the coat is poor from a previous diet, if the dog has a flea allergy problem or has suffered inherited or environmental effects that leave the coat looking far from good (dogs fed on raw natural food very rarely attract fleas, as their skin is less pleasant for parasites).

Raw, natural diets need consideration to ensure a variety of vitamins and minerals. Eggs are a good source of nutrients. Live yogurt has calcium. Cheese has many essential nutrients as well as being a good source of calcium, and most dogs love cheese. Meat can be varied, as tripe, beef, chicken, turkey and lamb are all easily available in wonderful little flat, easy-store freezer packs from most pet shops. Offal can be fed once a week.

Wheat is commonly used in dog food, but many dogs are allergic to this. Rice can be used along with lentils, peas, beans and chickpeas. Vegetables can be given to a dog with a free hand. Packs of mixed vegetables from the freezer at the supermarket are wonderful and easy to feed, and dogs love them – just give a handful a day to large dogs and a bit less to small dogs.

Dogs love fruit. Some like bananas, some like oranges. If the dog likes it, feed it – they usually know best. Certainly, they love blackberries and apples, and their mouth waters for raw cabbage and raw broccoli. However, it is best to avoid grapes, which are toxic to dogs.

Fats such as olive oil and peanut oil are nourishing, as are fish, brewer's yeast, kelp and dandelion. Fiber, such as oat bran, will help to prevent anal gland trouble. Cider vinegar is useful for the dog as well as us. It's good for arthritis and for helping the immune system. Extra vitamin C may be required where there is abnormal joint or bone development or weakness. Your veterinarian can advise you in this respect.

My dogs all look wonderful on a raw, natural diet and they have excellent coats.

COMPLETE FOOD

Dry, complete foods have a number of advantages. They are easily stored, quick and simple to feed, and clean. Most importantly, they provide a nutritionally complete diet, and so do all the hard work for you. Working out the dog's exact nutritional needs takes considerable research, and it is very easy to malnourish the dog accidentally.

There are several types of dry food on the market, but some are extremely high in protein, which does not suit all dogs. Indeed, excess protein has been known to make some dogs aggressive or hyperactive. Not all dogs of the same breed suit the same dry food, so take the advice of the breeder and/or your vet if you have any queries or concerns.

WORMING

If your dog has worms, its coat will suffer the consequences. Your breeder must supply you with details of when your new puppy was wormed and you must continue this process throughout your dog's life. Your vet will provide you with dosage details.

EXERCISE

Different breeds of dog vary enormously in their exercise requirement, but a fit and healthy dog will be recognized in an instant by the gleam of its jacket.

Healthy dogs obviously perform better than overweight or undernourished dogs. Young bones of the heavy breeds cannot take the strain of too much exercise and this is best kept to a minimum in such breeds as the Bernese or the Great Dane for instance, but moderate exercise will stimulate good health, which will show in the appearance of the coat. Exercise, walking, free-running and

Complete foods are quick and convenient, and provide all the nutrients a dog needs.

Regular exercise is essential for keeping a dog in peak fitness, and is reflected in its coat condition.

Where the dog is kept and what type of bed it has directly influences the appearance of its coat.

visits to new areas stimulate good health, and do the owner good too.

Do check your dog over carefully after a walk. Remove any burrs, grass seeds or other debris that may have accumulated. Check its feet too. In cold weather, check the pads for packed snow or ice, which can cause sores.

HOUSING

Where do you intend to keep your dog? This will depend largely on what breed you have. A Poodle, Cavalier King Charles Spaniel or Cocker Spaniel, for instance, will certainly live in the house at all times and probably sleep as near to you as possible, if not on the bed! A Bullmastiff, Bernese Mountain Dog, Newfoundland or Great Pyrenees may live in a utility room; an Alaskan Malamute may live in an outside kennel.

The bedding and housing you choose for your dog will have a bearing on the dog's coat. A dog that constantly lies on concrete

will wear the hair off its elbows and elsewhere. A dog lying on grass all the time may get bitten by insects or parasites and may develop skin irritations from the damp. Scratching at insect bites can also destroy a beautiful coat overnight.

Bedding should be washed regularly and floors should be kept clean, but remember that too strong a disinfectant can be dangerous if it comes into contact with the dog's skin or coat, particularly if it is licked off by the dog.

EARLY DETECTION

When regular attention is paid to grooming, early detection of problems like runny eyes, bad breath, skin disorders and allergies can be recognized and nipped in the bud (see Chapter Eight).

One flea sighted means that many more are present. Recognizing the first signs of a parasite invasion will not only save the dog from considerable discomfort and pain, it will also save you a great deal of money and a lot of distress.

Regular grooming allows you to quickly spot any health problems.

3 *ROUTINE CARE*

When should you start a grooming regime? From day one is the simple answer. Choose a suitable brush for your dog or puppy's coat type (see Chapter Six and Part Three), and spend a little time each day getting the dog used to being brushed.

For most breeds of dog, it is a simple task to put the puppy on a table and brush it. Even with the heavier breeds, it is useful to put the dog on a table to begin with, while carrying out routine brushing, combing, checking ears, eyes and mouth, as well as ensuring the anal area is clean and completely free of foreign matter or feces. Be particularly vigilant with heavy-coated breeds as they tend to collect debris, such as twigs, which must be removed before more clutter collects,

and the anal area must be kept scrupulously clean.

HOW OFTEN?

With a new puppy, it is worth brushing it on a daily basis. This interaction will benefit the puppy and teach it to respond to you and to observe house rules and manners. Grooming interaction will also help the puppy to feel secure, while you will learn more about the character you have chosen to live with for the coming years.

With some breeds that don't need constant attention to their coats, grooming may later become a weekly occupation rather than a daily one. However, it is wise to brush your puppy every day in the early weeks so that it gets used to being handled and to accepting being groomed.

EARLY TRAINING

It is essential to train the pup to stand still and to be groomed. If you don't get it used to the routine when it is young, it will be even harder when the dog is a full-grown adult.

Take the puppy to your chosen grooming spot, stand it up, say "Stand," wait for just a couple of seconds, then give it a treat and praise it handsomely. Repeat a few times every day, until the pup learns what the word "Stand" means. The treats, praise and cuddles

---

PROFESSIONAL GROOMING

For the average pet owner of the numerous breeds that require specific attention to their coats (e.g., the Poodle, Cocker Spaniel or most of the terrier breeds), a visit to a professional groomer will be necessary at regular intervals, from the age of about 3 to 4 months. However, basic daily brushing is all that is required for the average young pup and the adult dog alike.

Puppies should get used to the routine of grooming from a young age. This is particularly important with high-maintenance breeds, such as the Shih Tzu (right).

will make the dog look forward to its grooming times.

It is also useful to teach your dog to lie on its side while being groomed, particularly with longcoated breeds. It is a safe and comfortable position, and the dog should feel at ease.

Most puppies are pleased to have the attention of daily grooming. They love the interaction, and handling will be beneficial to their growth and mentality. With only a few minutes a day spent on grooming, the dog will become accustomed to being handled and will be more responsive to its owner or family.

With very young puppies, don't prolong

this session or the pup will become bored and will learn to hate the "boring" grooming sessions. Getting the pup used to being handled will prepare it for being handled by professional groomers, vets and show judges, and will mean it is generally happy and confident around all types of people.

One word of advice to the new puppy owner: check that your new young pup has relieved itself before grooming commences, so that it is not distracted. A pup that needs to urinate will object and whine all the time you are trying to brush it.

GETTING STARTED
Grooming incorporates the brushing, bathing, clipping or stripping of the dog's coat. The average dog owner rarely undertakes specialized or professional coat care. For the pet owner, it is sufficient to understand the rudiments of basic brushing and, depending on the breed of dog you have chosen, combing and bathing. This section is intended for the novice, or the new dog owner.

PUPPY POWER

When grooming puppies, lay a thick towel on the grooming table. This will make it more comfortable for the pup, and it is less likely to become restless.

Brushing a dog on a table is far more convenient and less backbreaking than trying to see to its needs while kneeling on the floor. Dogs are usually far better behaved while on a table.

- Place the puppy on the grooming table, and stand close by, with a finger holding its collar to ensure that the dog does not fall or jump off the table.
- Tell the puppy to "Stand," and praise and reassure it when it stands quietly.
- Commence brushing with your free hand, starting from the head and working systematically down the body, legs and tail.
- Do this for a minute or two, then tell the pup to "Turn" as you turn the pup the opposite way round.
- Again, tell the pup to "Stand" and commence brushing this side, starting with the head and working across.
- Stroke the coat firmly but gently, and repeat the word "Stand" every now and

It is important to play with your puppy after grooming, so the dog learns to view it as a rewarding experience.

then. Praise and reassure the pup intermittently.
- When you have finished brushing the coat, reward the pup with praise and its favorite tidbit.
- Then lift the pup down onto the floor, and play a game together.
- The puppy will soon look forward to its grooming sessions because they are so enjoyable.
- After a couple of days, when the pup is accustomed to being handled in this way, progress to using a comb after brushing where the coat necessitates this (see Part Three for details).

OTHER CHECKS
Your puppy should also get used to being checked all over – ears, teeth and nails need special attention (see Chapter Seven). Not only will this make your life easier in the long term (your adult will be more compliant), but your vet will thank you for not having a ticklish, nervous or aggressive dog.

Grooming at waist height is far more comfortable for the handler.

When choosing a groomer, ask to watch them at work before giving them your business.

very arthritic and I always trimmed him with this in mind. He never once attempted to snap at me.

You should ask the groomer if they have ever been bitten, and how often. I am always wary, for instance, when I talk to groomers at seminars and they say, "I hate doing Poodles, they are nasty, snappy things." If they can't get on with the tolerant Poodle, well...

However, we must not assume this is the norm; most groomers do care and are passionately devoted to their job, growing to love the dogs they trim on a regular basis.

In the U.S., you should ask if the groomer is licensed or certified. Some states require that the shop is licensed, not the groomer. Some require that the groomer is licensed to handle pesticides.

SEEING IS BELIEVING

If you are impressed by a groomer, ask to stay and watch some dogs being groomed. If you are pleased with what you see (i.e. that the dogs are happy and relaxed, and that the groomer is confident and skilled), make an appointment for your dog to be groomed, and ask if you can watch. No groomer with confidence in his or her own ability will

object to this request by the owner.

It has to be said that some dogs play up a bit to begin with if their owners are present. But if the owner ignores the dog and just sits quietly, the dog will soon settle.

Some groomers are happy for clients to watch their work, but are not keen on them being present when their own dogs are groomed – because of the time factor in getting the pet to settle. Consider your own dog's character and talk to your groomer to reach a compromise.

IMPORTANT INFORMATION

The groomer should request and record specific information from you. Besides your name and one or more phone numbers at which to reach you, they should ask your pet's age, the name and number of your veterinarian, and any specific health problems (e.g., moles or allergies).

SUCCESSFUL RELATIONSHIP

It is very important to take your puppy to see the groomer at the earliest possible date, even for a brush, so that the dog will become accustomed to being handled by the groomer at a young age. This will not only help the groomer, it will help your dog and prevent it from getting into a neglected and matted state. The moment the coat becomes matted, the more uncomfortable it will be for the dog to be groomed – the dog will then associate the groomer with discomfort and will be less cooperative on future visits.

Often, problems occur because the owner doesn't think about taking the pup for professional grooming until it is more than a year old, or until the time comes when they can no longer cope with the mats that have formed in the coat. Of course, this makes the dog's first experience of being professionally trimmed less enjoyable than it should be, which can lead to problems later on.

ACCIDENTS HAPPEN

Do check that the groomer has adequate insurance coverage before you take your dog in to be groomed. Accidents rarely occur in the grooming parlor, but there will be the odd occasion where an accident will take place no matter how careful the groomer is.

Most pet owners' insurance covers such eventualities in the event of the groomer being personally uninsured, but it may be advisable to check this out with your own policy to be on the safe side. As well, you may injure your own dog and need veterinary help, so be sure that you are covered.

HOW MUCH WILL IT COST?

By the time this book is published, prices will have changed, but I can give you some helpful pointers. The cost of having a dog professionally groomed varies according to the breed and the work involved. For example, American Cockers take longer than English Cockers, as a rule. The following factors will also be taken into account:

• Whether the dog is clipped or stripped (hand-stripping takes far longer).
• Whether or not the dog is having a bath.
• The condition of the coat.
• The trim – all cut off, "Lamb," "Dutch," "Lion," etc.
• The geographical region (although this is now leveling out with the increasing membership of association bodies).

If you choose to own a coated breed of dog, such as a terrier, Afghan, Old English Sheepdog or Poodle, you will periodically have to take your pet to a groomer for a haircut, bath or professional groom. Hopefully, you will have considered professional coat care costs before purchasing your puppy.

Although they may look similar, the American Cocker Spaniel (below) takes longer to groom than the English Cocker (left) – something that should be reflected in your pricing structure.

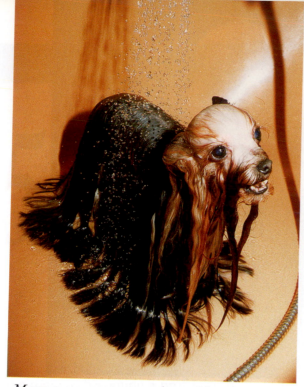

Many groomers start out by working from home, but sharing the family bathroom with your canine clients is not a good long-term plan!

groomers set up a business from home, even using a spare bedroom and their personal bathroom to wash dogs. This may suffice for a while, but can be impractical and does not give a professional impression. In the long term, you should consider either finding business premises or building an extension to the home where the facilities are more convenient and hygienic.

How much you charge for your services will have to take account of expenses, or you will end up working hard for nothing. All aspects must be considered, such as rent, electricity costs, insurance, equipment and your time. Also, setting up a business requires a certain amount of advertising, which never comes cheap.

However, using your talent will help cut costs. If you or a friend has a computer, it is relatively easy to produce your own business cards and to design and make fliers, which can be given out to pet shops, etc. Advertising in the local newspaper is probably a must to start with, and an advertising telephone directory serves as a good shop window. Eventually, word-of-mouth recommendations should provide most of your business.

ASSESSING THE COMPETITION

Research how many groomers are covering your area. Realistically, is there room for another? What services do they offer? What prices do they charge?

Where groomers have set up businesses at home and have no major overhead, they can, of course, charge less for what they are doing or make a bigger profit. Cutting costs because others in the area are not charging enough may prove fatal for the groomer who has invested a large sum in equipment and needs to pay rent. There are only so many dogs any one person can do in a day and if you are breaking even or working at a loss, it's really not worth the effort.

Belonging to a professional trade body or association may be an added expense, but it does provide a guide to the prices charged throughout the country. Often, geographical location may determine price, and vary considerably.

Another way of finding out about prices in your area is to call local groomers and ask what they charge. Not all groomers are skilled on all breeds so they may well charge less for, say, a Poodle because they are better on terriers, or vice versa.

If your competitors are good at trimming, and cheap, you may have to consider if you will get enough business not only to survive, but to pay the mortgage. If the geographical area does not look viable, consider another.

Note: in the U.S., it is illegal to discuss pricing as a group.

INSURANCE

There are insurance companies that have specific packages for the groomer. Being self-employed, anything could happen. I once heard of a groomer who had a puppy hooked to the wall. She went away to answer the telephone, the dog tried to jump off the table, and strangled itself with its own lead. This would never have happened if the

With time, word-of-mouth recommendations will help to build your reputation.

groomer had had proper training on safety.

Another groomer had a car accident and had to dissolve her business overnight when she was unable to work for six months. These may be extreme cases, but accidents can happen and for just a little expense a year, you can be covered for all eventualities.

ACCOUNTS

It is a good idea to start keeping a strict order of accounts from day one. If you do not have computer skills (there are some very simple accounting packages), it is relatively easy to keep two books in order:

- One book for your expenses (telephone expenses, gas, clothes, equipment).
- Another book for your income – any earnings you make.
- If you decide to venture into adding some retail to your business (e.g., selling grooming products), keeping an accurate inventory is essential.

It is also essential either to have a professional accountant or to undertake self-assessment for tax purposes. Your local tax office will have details.

water before they are applied to the coat. It is always good policy to use a quality shampoo, and the milder the better. Most groomers have a selection of shampoos in the salon from which to choose the best one for each individual dog.

Some of the latest shampoos and conditioners are the "silver" and "diamond" types to make white dogs look sparkling, removing stains and discoloration from all or parts of the coat. Another recent trend is the special skin- and coat-purifying shampoos and masks that can be used occasionally for a healthier look and a superb finish.

"Sculpture rinses" for scissored and trimmed dogs are a must for the groomer who wishes to achieve an outstanding finish with both pet and show dogs.

CONDITIONERS

These are not necessary for all coats, but most (whether long, short, wiry or curly) will benefit from the use of oil-based enhancers to help to keep mats at bay.

Some conditioners are designed to improve the finish of scissored breeds; mostly, they are concentrated and should be diluted with water when required (always check the product label first).

Conditioners vary from a conditioning "sleek rinse" for long, lustrous coats to dematting cream rinses with anti-static properties, and "crinkle-beaters" (to straighten hair), which give a fantastic straight blow-dry.

Use oil-based conditioners sparingly or you may end up with a very greasy dog.

COLOR-ENHANCING

Another aspect of beautifying the dog is to have the coat color-enhanced. This is usually accomplished by using shampoos to bring out the natural coloring in the dog's coat – black for black dogs, blue for blue and silver dogs, extra-white shampoo for white coats (and parts of the coat, such as a Collie mane). There is no colorant in these shampoos – they simply emphasize the dog's existing color.

DRYERS

These are essential. It is always a good policy to have a hands-free, powerful, specially made dog dryer. There are several on the market. Because I love "one-to-one" interaction with the dog while I am grooming, I do not use cage-dryers (below), but they are readily available and a busy establishment may find these contraptions useful and maybe necessary.

There are also revolutionary dryers that are credited as being the ultimate in the drying experience, combining a tremendous airflow with heat for instant dying. They are thermostatically controlled and economical to use, and come with a stand for a hands-free operation. However, they do not appeal to all dogs – some hate the strong force of these dryers, and object.

AUTOMATIC DOG DRYER

An automatic dog dryer is a cabinet in which the dog is placed in warm air. It is sometimes described as a "cage-dryer." This dryer is thermostatically controlled and economical to use. The cage-dryer may be useful for German Shepherd Dogs and shorthaired breeds where blow-drying is not essential.

STAND DRYER

This is a powerful and robust dryer with a rotating nozzle – a favorite with exhibitors when presentation is a priority. It allows you to have both your hands free to brush and handle the dog.

HAND DRYERS

There are also several hand-held dryers available, and they are sometimes useful, especially for those groomers who trim dogs in their own home and do not want to haul a large dryer around with them.

POWER BLOWER/GROOMER

Modern methods and equipment will save the groomer from hours of work and from getting sore fingers. The power groomer is a highly effective blower that penetrates and separates every section of the hair, removing dust and tangles, and blowing the hair straight.

When the dog needs to be brushed prior to being bathed, the power blower can be used instead, provided the dog has no objection to the jet of air. Dogs soon get used to this piece of equipment and most dogs enjoy the invigorating action. Make sure dogs have cotton batting in their ears to protect from the noise.

Between baths, too, the power groomer can be used as a means of grooming the coat. Blow the hair away from the skin to remove dust and curls that may develop into tangles. This technique takes only a few minutes, and reduces the actual brushing time by many minutes. This is especially useful in breeds such as the Old English Sheepdog, which sometimes has a coat that mats by the minute!

Wetting a matted dog will severely exacerbate the problem because water tends to encourage hair to stick like glue to the mats; then, if the dog is not dried with great care, the situation gets worse as the coat shrinks into the mat and you end up with one big felt. (However, there is a three-stage grooming product that allows you to put even the most matted dog directly into the tub, and removes mats with ease. Contact your grooming supplier for information.)

A slicker brush is particularly useful for thick coats.

Novice groomers often get into a panic when trying to cope with a coat that has matted solid after a bath. The secret is to prevent this action by carefully analyzing the situation before you start grooming. Use the power blower, without heat, to separate each section of the coat, and also spray in de-tangle spray if the coat is dry.

TOWELS
Superabsorbent towels are a great asset for getting excess water from the dog before you start with the dryer. Consisting of a quality drying cloth that is hard-wearing, easy to clean and reusable, these superabsorbent towels soak up huge amounts of water and come in standard and large sizes.

COMBS
It would not be feasible to list every single comb, so a selection has been chosen.

COARSE
This comb has stainless steel teeth and a round handle for eliminating clogging (i.e., matting or felting).

MEDIUM
This is useful in eliminating clogging.

MEDIUM/COARSE
A chrome, all-metal comb with a rounded back for comfort.

UNTANGLE PET COMB
Features teeth that rotate 360 degrees and gently turn to remove tangles fast and without too much pain.

MOLTING COMBS
Coarse and medium combs, with stainless steel teeth, a white plastic handle and a round-shaped back. These combs virtually eliminate clogging.

BACK COMB
For styling and creating lift.

TAIL COMB
For separating and parting the coat.

FLEA COMB
Has very fine teeth to help remove parasites.

BRUSHES

PIN AND BRISTLE BRUSHES
Natural bristle brushes come in large, medium and small – with a cushioned pad.

A good pair of clippers and a variety of blades will be needed.

SLICKER BRUSH
These come in a variety of sizes and styles (universal, curved or with a straight back). Each brush has hooked steel pins to break up the tangles. Every groomer should have these.

CLIPPERS AND BLADES

AESCULAP FAVORITA II
A favorite with busy, professional groomers, this is cool-running and powerful when tackling neglected and felted coats. Blades range from GT703 1/10 mm as a surgical blade, GT712 1 mm for short precision work, GT742 2 mm for matted thick coats, GT758 5 mm for general purpose body, GT770 7 mm for winter, and up to GT784 16 mm for a very long coat (with a range of blades in between).

ANDIS CORDLESS
A professional cordless clipper with a battery, which can take Oster blades.

The Andis AG is a durable professional clipper that is easy to handle and quiet-running. Blades range from No. 50 for surgical, right through to No. 10 for face, No. 7 for body and up to No. 3.75 for very long.

OSTER
This two-speed clipper is a professional tool with Andis-compatible blades.

The Oster A5 clipper is a true friend of the trainee or student, as well as the experienced groomer because it is gentle on the dog. However, you must check it frequently to ensure the blade is not running hot.

Blades include:

• No. 40: surgical
• No. 30: used for clipping Poodle feet
• No. 15: a face blade
• No. 10: used where the skin is more delicate or where the hair is less thick on the face, such as on a white Poodle
• No. 5: summer body
• No. 4F: for a long finish.

BLADE BANK
A "blade bank" holds up to 15 blades, so they can each be identified easily.

CLIPPER OIL
Lubricant for blades and scissors is essential.

BLADE WASH
A degreasing, cleaning substance for blades.

GREASE
For clipper bearings.

COMB ATTACHMENTS
Check that they suit your type of clipper. Use for changing the size of the blade to leave a specific length of coat. Useful where owners like an inch or two of coat left on.

EAR CARE
Forceps, ear cleaner and ear powder are assets in the grooming room.
See page 51.

EYE CARE
Tear-stain remover and emollient are available

to aid a clean finish, and to help remove eye stains caused by tears (see page 60).

NAIL CARE
There are several types of nail clippers available, some of which include a safety guard to prevent too much nail being clipped off at a time. They come in small, medium and large sizes. The guillotine and scissor-types, with or without plastic-coated handles, are a matter of preference, but buy the best quality you can, as these tend to be smoother and easier to use. Some of the cheaper versions have ragged edges which can cut your fingers, so beware.

Permanganate crystals should also be on hand, should the quick of the nail be nicked. Tip a small amount into a saucer and dip some damp cotton batting into it. This should stop the bleeding (see page 50).

SCISSORS
There are literally hundreds of types of scissors on the market, ranging from the very expensive high-standard finishing scissors, which give a truly expert cut, to the more affordable, basic varieties.

The type of finish and the job at hand will determine which scissors are used. Generally, groomers use small scissors for clipping the hair between spaniels' feet, etc. Some people use the same pair of scissors for everything, even slicing through mats. I keep certain finishing scissors for show dogs, and use a different pair for general scissoring.

Some groomers prefer scissors with a finger guide – a rubber insert or a hook for the little finger, to prevent the scissors from moving or slipping while in use. Others prefer no finger guides.

At most shows, and at grooming seminars, it is possible to try out several different types of scissors, taking note of the job for which they are recommended. Remember, high price does not necessarily always mean a super finish.

Always try out any scissors you are considering purchasing – one pair may be a perfect fit for one person, but may slip in another's hand. In grooming school, you should be taught how to use scissors properly.

Thinning scissors are often used on spaniels and thick coats.

THINNING SCISSORS

Thinning scissors have a flat blade on one side and a blade with gaps on the other. They are used primarily on spaniels and thick coats that need thinning out rather than clipping off.

STRIPPING TOOLS

There are several tools available, used for various aspects of stripping different coats.

STRIPPING KNIFE

Left- and right-handed, the knife comes with a long, fine blade with a round, bobbled end. It can be used for carding (see page 48), and can be obtained in different sizes.

STRIPPING STONES

These are gray stones that some groomers use for stripping. They can be cut to size, and are used alongside – or instead of – the groomer's finger and thumb, or stripping knife.

DOG DRESSER

This is used for stripping, and comes with blades, as opposed to the "fixed knife" where the stripping blade is attached all in one.

A stripping stone helps to remove loose coats.

DEMATTING TOOLS

THE MAT-SPLITTER

This is an effective aid that cuts through mats and tangles with ease. It is simple to use, causing the dog very little distress, even with the toughest knots. The handle is shaped for comfort, has a tapered guide and has a honed steel cutting blade that penetrates the toughest of tangles.

MAT-BREAKER

This is scientifically designed for easy and efficient removal of mats and tangles with minimum hair loss. The stainless-steel blades are shaped for optimum effect, and the blades are replaceable.

DEMATTING RAKE

This comes in different sizes and can be reversed from right to left. This tool has replaceable serrated stainless-steel blades.

CLEANING PRODUCTS

You will also need some pet-safe disinfectants for cleaning your equipment, tools, floors, and so on. Your grooming supplier should have a good selection to choose from.

A stripping knife is useful for terrier coats if hand-stripping is not performed.

BENEATH THE COAT

Whether you merely intend to groom your own pet dog or you wish to become a top award-winning groomer, you should understand a little about the dog and its structure.

The following diagram is of the canine skeleton. It doesn't matter if it is not correct for your breed (obviously it looks nothing like a Corgi or a Dachshund); the bones are all present in every dog we see, whatever the breed (the only exception being the Norwegian Lundehund, which has six toes on each of his four feet).

THE SKELETON

The skeleton of the dog is relevant to the groomer, especially when a dog's breed standard advises trimming to a certain point (such as the hock). Groomers who familiarize themselves with at least the more obvious points of the body (e.g., stifle) can follow grooming instructions with confidence.

The detailed breed profiles in Part Three sometimes refer to particular parts of the dog, and it will be useful if you refer back to this diagram when reading them.

PET OR SHOW?

The professional groomer has to ascertain whether they are working on a pet dog or a show dog. There are many wonderful aids and coat-enhancing properties that are great for a pet, but which may be considered illegal substances in the show ring. The use of them may break the rules of some countries' national kennel clubs.

In North America, for instance, many breeds are prepared for the show ring by incorporating clipping and coat aids such as hair spray. That same technique may be classed as breaking the rules according, say, to the British Kennel Club.

However, preparation for the show ring or for conformation purposes does not, in general, fall to the average grooming salon to undertake, as most handlers prepare the dogs themselves. But, do ask the owner if the dog is likely to be shown. Remember – it is better to be safe than sorry.

Coat-enhancing materials, such as chalk or specialist shampoos, can be used on pet dogs, but show dogs should generally be kept natural.

Also, while clipping a pet terrier is perfectly permissible and saves hours of work, it is not the thing to do to a show dog, as it will take months and months before the dog can be shown again.

BEST TOOLS

Care should be taken to use the correct brush when brushing the dog. Even the skin of thick-coated breeds can be made red raw by a heavy-handed groomer who drags through the coat with too much vigor, scratching the skin. Don't use a slicker or steel pin brush on skin that has been clipped, especially on delicate parts, such as the face. It is inexcusable to graze the dog's skin in this way. Use a soft brush for these parts, if indeed they need to be brushed at all.

For more information on equipment, see Chapter Six.

MAT MATTERS

Undercoat, as seen in dogs like the Old English Sheepdog, can mat solid against the skin and become a horrendous task to remove. Inexperienced groomers have been known to bathe a dog full of matted undercoat or felted clogs of hair and then put the dog in a drying cabinet or cage. Once

dry, the top hair is then brushed to make the dog look fluffy. The dog looks good on the surface, but the full story beneath the topcoat is quite a different matter.

If the dog is bathed when matted, the shampoo will generally get clogged into the mats, making the situation even more disastrous. Many pet owners bathe their dogs between trims and leave them to dry, making the job of grooming far more difficult. The dog may be clean, but its coat is not in good condition and is certainly not free of tangles. Explaining the problem to the owner and how to avoid it can help to avert future problems.

No dog can look or feel its best unless all tangles, mats and felts are removed from the coat. When a dog has a badly matted coat, it is advisable to spray in a dematter or untangle lotion and leave it to soak for 10 minutes or so before using a slicker brush or mat-breaker to remove the offending sections.

Regular brushing will prevent mats, but if they are already established and cannot be removed, then clipping the dog is in its best interest.

If dematting the dog will be considered torturous to the animal, then the hair must be cut or clipped off. No groomer must be responsible for causing any dog severe distress. Discuss the problem with the owner, explaining that you have no wish to act in a cruel manner and that you will use clippers on the dog if necessary, rather than inflict needless pain. Saving some of the matting to show the owner can be effective.

PREBATH CLIPPING

Some dogs, such as a hairy Poodle or an Old English Sheepdog, can have a great deal of their thick coat clipped before a bath.

Admittedly, clipping clean hair is less wearing on clipper blades, but, with the use of an easy-clip lubricating spray and oil, there shouldn't be too much to worry about, and it will cut down washing and drying time by nearly half – less electricity, less time, less stress for the dog, more economy all around!

The clipping of some parts, such as the hairy feet of a spaniel, will shorten the drying time, but do clean your blades after clipping between feet or they will clog with debris, such as mud, sand and hair. Remember not to clip wet hair. Using a fine blade, it is relatively easy on the dog to clip the fiercely matted hair between some dogs' feet.

The same goes for dogs that are matted solid around the rear end. Clip over the anus area (but not the bulbous anus itself) with a medium-cut blade, being careful to hold the dog's genitals for protection. This will get rid of a lot of unwanted hair and debris that it is pointless bathing, drying or trying to comb out.

In hairy or matted pet dogs, it is often a good idea to clip out all the hair underneath the tummy, groin area and chest, right up to the dog's rib cage and sometimes between its front legs, underneath the arms. This procedure prevents matting and keeps the dog smelling fresher. When the dog is standing, the clipped hair is not noticeable and will only be seen when the dog rolls over onto its back to show you its nice clean stomach. Of course, this would never be done to a show dog.

Prebath clipping can save on washing and drying time.

BATHING

ESSENTIAL EQUIPMENT

Grooming techniques are getting ever more sophisticated, and we now have numerous coat aids, sprays, selective shampoos and incredible conditioners to help us turn out a first-class job.

Some aromatherapy shampoos, made from natural therapeutic organic compounds that nourish the coat and skin, are wonderful to use, and they produce a top-quality finish.

One essential for the bath is a long, secure rubber mat to prevent the dog from slipping. Also, it is impossible to cope without a decent hose spray to distribute the water evenly throughout.

PROCEDURE

Before we begin, remember that you should never leave a dog unattended. Some people think the dog is safe if it is restrained on a grooming table or in the bath, hooked on a frame or tied up. Dogs have hung themselves in a matter of seconds when groomers have made the horrendous mistake of leaving the dog unattended. Your customers are your responsibility and you should never leave them, even for a second.

When putting a large dog into a waist-high bath, it is a good idea to get assistance rather than break your back. Another way around the problem is to walk the dog up a ramp. Then place its front paws on the bath, lift up the back end and tip the dog in, or have the table placed next to the bath and encourage the dog to step into the bath from this height. Most dogs are fairly obliging, especially when they are used to visiting the groomer.

Posing more of a problem are the 100-pound (45 kg) heavyweights that are four years old and have never been on a table or had a bath in their life. These dogs tend to panic on initiation, but, with careful handling, they can be encouraged to respond and settle down – and may actually enjoy the experience!

Some people have hooks in the wall above the bath and clip the dog's leash to this in order to keep it still; however, some dogs react to this and are best left to stand of their own accord.

Sometimes, with a large breed that is not used to the bath, two people are better than one – one at the head, one at the other end. It makes the task twice as quick, so is economical in time.

WETTING THE COAT

The dog should be thoroughly wetted before a shampoo is applied. Lift long hair to be certain of getting right down to the roots. Anybody who has had a dreadful hairwash from an inexperienced junior hairdresser will know how itchy the scalp feels after hair has been insufficiently wetted.

It is not advisable to stand dogs in a pool of dirty water, so make sure the water drains away as it runs off the dog.

Use a decent water spray at all times, with the temperature set to warm. Test the water on the delicate underside of your arm, not on your hands, which are hardened to the elements.

Start with the head. The dog's ears may need to be protected with cotton batting to prevent water getting into them. Wet down the neck, along the back and down the left side (including the legs). Then repeat on the right side, turning the dog only if necessary (turning the dog at this stage will encourage it to jump out, so be warned). Lastly, wet the tail.

If the dog is very sensitive about having its head wet, then start with the tail and work up the body, wetting the head last.

APPLYING SHAMPOO

Now work the diluted shampoo through the

ROUTINE FOR BATHING

1. Wet the coat thoroughly with warm (not hot) water. Part the hair to check that the water has penetrated down to the skin.

2. If a dog is sensitive about having its head wet, be particularly gentle around this area, and wet the head last – just before applying the shampoo.

3. Apply the shampoo and lather down to the skin. Be careful not to get any soap into the dog's eyes.

4. Rinse thoroughly – any soap left in the coat will cause intense itchiness.

5. Dry the head first to make the dog comfortable.

6. Work along the body, using a superabsorbent towel to remove most of the moisture.

coat with your hands. Shampoo is rarely put straight onto the dog without being mixed with a certain amount of water to help distribute it and prevent it from affecting the skin.

Massage the shampoo into the coat thoroughly, not forgetting the area underneath the chest and stomach, the anal area and the dog's feet. Make sure the shampoo gets down to the skin and is well lathered, adding water if required.

With the head area, you must be careful not to get shampoo in the dog's eyes. Rinse immediately if there is a suspicion of this happening. Do not put shampoo into the dog's ears at any time.

Rinse off the shampoo and use a second application if required. With experience, you will be able to feel when the coat is clean – it will "squeak" when clean, as human hair does.

RINSING

Rinsing should be thorough – rinse, rinse, rinse until the coat feels squeaky clean. Any shampoo left in the coat will cause flaking scurf, felting and intense itching. Some makes of shampoo claim to be mild, but are too strong for the dog's sensitive skin and may also cause the dog to itch. Use a very mild, natural-ingredient shampoo on particularly sensitive skin or with dogs suffering from an allergy.

With shortcoated dogs, such as the Dalmatian or Weimaraner, a thorough brushing with a hound glove when in the bath will remove a lot of dead and molting hair. The dog will dry smoother and quicker, and the owner will be delighted that far less hair comes out on their carpet.

DRYING

Water can be removed from the coat while the dog is still in the bath. Squeeze out the excess moisture with cotton towels or super-absorbent towels.

DEMATTING CONDITIONER

Dematting conditioners can be a godsend on some tangly coats. Brush them through the entire coat when the hair is wet, and the tangles unwind or loosen enough to be brushed and combed out. This is done before the drying commences, and most dematters should be rinsed out. Check the directions on the label.

Some breeds, like the St. Bernard and the heavy-coated spitz breeds, will benefit from having water blasted from the coat with a high-velocity dryer (see page 31). Do this by placing the dog on the grooming table and holding a superabsorbent towel behind the dog to catch the water. Then use a power blower on the coat before placing the dog in the drying cabinet or finishing off with the blow-dryer.

This method of removing excess water from the coat is not a good idea with dogs that need blow-drying, such as the show Poodle, as the hair would become dry too quickly and may crinkle and curl, hampering scissoring.

If a "stay-in-the-coat" spray conditioner is required, then apply this before drying commences, as recommended in the manufacturer's instructions. With coated dogs, such as the Poodle, it is essential to blow-dry the hair by separating the strands with the aid of a slicker or pin brush and using a power dryer to blow the hair.

Each small section must be parted, usually starting from the back foot and systematically working upwards. Be careful not to have the air blow directly onto the skin, as this would be too hot for the dog to endure, and it would react by trying to run away from the burning sensation. Blow the hair away from the skin, but do not blow the skin itself.

Most dogs hate the blower on their faces,

PROCEDURE

Use a fine-rubber hygiene glove and absorbent paper towel, and place your finger and thumb on either side of the anus. You will be able to feel the hardened gland about 1 inch (2.5 cm) in. Press in, up and outwards to expel the vile-smelling fluid, which is sometimes almost as thick as toothpaste, and sometimes as liquid as water.

There is a knack to this and some dogs' glands are far easier to empty than others. If the area is very sensitive or smelly, or both, and nothing comes away, it is as well to advise the client to take the dog to the vet to have this area checked out in case something more sinister has developed.

NAILS

Once the dog is bathed (before or after drying the coat) and is sitting on the table, this is a good time to trim back your dog's nails, as they are softened by the water and are usually easier, and less brittle, to snip. Some dogs have long blood vessels in their nails because the nails have not been trimmed back on a regular basis since puppyhood, and very little nail can be cut. Using a large file or an electric file is often safer in these cases.

Trim the nails after a bath, when they will be softer and easier to cut.

However, electric filers often wind themselves up in long, loose coats. Breeds such as the Afghan or the American Cocker should be manually filed.

The "quick" is the nerve and blood supply in the nail. If this is cut, it will be very painful to the dog, and may become infected. Stop bleeding using a styptic pencil or permanganate crystals. Care should be taken with nails; it causes the dog severe pain when the quick is cut.

If the nails of a nervous or ticklish dog need cutting, then arrange for somebody to hold the dog and talk to it while you quickly carry out the task. Often, such dogs can have their nails filed without objection.

DEWCLAWS

Dewclaws are a problem in some active dogs because they can easily get torn away from the foot. Some dogs, such as the Poodle, have dewclaws removed at birth, while others, such as the Great Pyrenees, have a breed standard that requires these extra toes.

Dewclaws should be checked on a regular basis, as the nail can grow and grow, and may even grow back into the leg. This causes considerable pain to the dog and can result in infections, to the point where surgery is the only answer.

In the pet dog, dewclaws are not required at all. If they have been left on, they cannot be removed unless by a major operation. The nail of the dewclaw, however, can be clipped back with the rest of the nails. The less roadwork the dog does, the more likely it is that the nails will regularly need cutting or filing back (at least every three months).

Some dogs have poor feet, where the nails turn before they reach the ground. Such dogs will need their nails to be clipped back more often than others.

Check the dewclaws every week when you look at your dog's nails. Puppies that have

1. Brush the hair around the ears, and expose the ear opening.

2. Use forceps to gently remove hair from the ear.

3. Apply a proprietary ear cleaner to a cotton pad.

4. Wipe around the outer ear.

dewclaws need to have these clipped at the same time as you cut their sharp little needle-like nails.

EARS

Holding the ear flap back, clean the ears with alcohol or ear cleaner if necessary and apply ear powder to ensure the ear stays healthy and mite-free. After applying ear powder and leaving it in for a few minutes, use forceps to clean the hair from the ear, removing tiny bits of hair at a time. This will be less painful than using fingers.

Make sure that you clean the forceps with alcohol before and after each dog, to ensure that you do not spread infection or mites. See also page 59.

EYES

Keep the eyes clean, checking routinely for any sleep deposits or any weeping ducts. Use damp cotton batting to remove any accumulation or this will form a hard lump and could develop into a sore. See page 59.

TEETH

A dog's teeth should be routinely checked when visiting a professional groomer so early

Hormone imbalances can cause bald patches, particularly on the sides, around the waist area. This is different from sebaceous adenitis and can be treated by a vet.

WARTS

These can cause severe discomfort, or else a dog can be covered with endless extrusions and not seem to feel a thing. Trying to clip a dog that has several warts hidden under a matted coat is a nightmare. The tops can be clipped off unintentionally and the bleeding can be quite worrying.

Some breeds seem to suffer more than others. Norwegian Elkhounds seem to have a particular problem with open cysts and wart extrusions, as do Cockers and Toy Poodles. Sometimes, these unwanted skin deformities are as hard as stone and grow in odd shapes to amazing lengths, when they may break off with no bleeding taking place. It is advisable to check thick and matted coats for warts and cysts – a groomer's worst headache.

Older dogs seem particularly prone to warts and can get quite touchy about being trimmed. It must be quite painful to have these extrusions cut or knocked off.

Treatment: Consult your vet if your dog develops warts – in some cases, the vet will remove them. Some people believe that banana skin, gently rubbed against the wart three times a day, is effective. Where the wart is inflamed or weeping, a vet should be consulted without delay.

COMMON PROBLEMS

ANAL SACS

The anal sacs, located under the skin near the anus, are two pouches that release fluid when the dog defecates; this fluid is used for identification among dogs.

If the sacs do not empty, they become blocked and may smell or become uncomfortable to the dog. The area around the anus may be swollen and puffy, indicating that the anal sacs require emptying.

Emptying anal sacs is a skilled job, and you are advised to seek help from a professional groomer or a vet. For more information, see page 49.

BEARDS

Bearded mouths cause many a headache. They collect debris with great ease, and woe to any owner who fails to remove twigs and general debris from a long beard. Once it is matted in, and this takes very little time, it is incredibly difficult to remove. Sometimes the only salvation is to cut the beard short, which is not an ideal option, particularly for owners of breeds like the Schnauzer, for whom the beard is a distinguishing characteristic.

Beards can collect everyday debris, such as food, and can stain easily.

EAR PROBLEMS

Erect-eared dogs (such as the German Shepherd Dog), and those with pendulous ears (such as the Basset Hound) are equally at risk of ear problems.

Ear infections seem to be ongoing and difficult to clear up. It is said that the ear is a perfect place for infection to flourish. As there is high humidity, the ear easily collects debris, moisture and dust, which provides the perfect environment for bacteria. No two dogs are alike, and a little bit of dust and hair in one ear can cause many ongoing problems, yet nothing at all in another ear.

It is a good idea to check the ears on a regular basis and to clean out the offending excess hair and wax (see page 51). Equally, overzealous ear cleaning can aggravate the situation, so it is a matter of getting the right balance. Ear problems should always initially be investigated by a veterinarian, as allergies are a prime cause of ear infections, and low thyroid levels can also be responsible for chronic problems.

Mites, which are very often carried unseen by cats, can invade a dog's ears. Early detection is best. There is frequently a brown, smelly discharge from the ear and sometimes red sores and inflammation are obvious. In cases of mite invasion, ask your vet for a suitable ear treatment.

Be extra vigilant in autumn when there is the danger of grass seeds working their way into the ear.

SNOODS

Pendulous ears get everywhere, as those with spaniels will confirm. Dogs love sniffing, and when their noses go down to pick up a scent, so do their long ears. Many owners wrap their dog's ears to prevent them getting too dirty. "Snoods" (home-knitted or made from old pantyhose) can be used to pull over the dog's head to keep its ears free of dirt while out walking, or to keep the ears from tipping into the dog's dinner while eating.

Snoods should not be used all the time, though, as they cover the ear canal and prevent fresh air from keeping the ear dry and healthy. They should be used only at meal and exercise times.

EYE PROBLEMS

Some dogs inherit eye abnormalities, which cause their eyes to water constantly, and which cause brown stains. A puppy's eyes often water during teething.

Entropion, where the eyelashes turn inwards, is a common cause of eye-watering, but sometimes infections are responsible. All cases should be seen by a vet to ascertain the cause.

Clean the eyes carefully with a wet cotton pad, using separate pads for each eye, and making sure any debris buildup in the corner of the eye is removed.

Some breeds are prone to weepy eyes and tear stains, and need regular eye care.

Most dogs learn to accept grooming – and even enjoy the attention.

"DIFFICULT" DOGS

Unfortunately, through lack of time, skill or understanding, some groomers can make a dog react in a defensive way, which then means the dog is labeled as nasty. The only thing to blame here is the groomer's lack of training or experience. A spoiled brat of a dog is sometimes awkward to begin with, but dogs hate being ignored, so if you don't say much to them and don't take on their owners' "baby talk," the dogs soon pester you for attention.

Some dogs, who have been mistreated or misunderstood, will be difficult to trim for four or five visits to an experienced, flexible and well-trained groomer. Then they suddenly become angels. This is common, far more common than the dog that can't be won round by patience and kind handling.

Dogs with arthritis or puppies with growing pains should have their situation assessed and taken into consideration. Again, experience and good training allows the groomer to recognize these problems and act accordingly.

Dogs bite through self-defense and because they are worried or scared and feel vulnerable. Act confidently, treating the dog with respect and kindness at all times. If a dog is nervous, talk to it to reassure it.

Some dogs are aggressive because they consider themselves to be dominant over people. With such cases, the owner should enrole the dog at a good obedience class or seek specialist behavioral advice.

A new groomer, a lady with three weeks' training, proudly told me how she had fought with a 7-month-old Standard Poodle for more than an hour to clean the hair from its ears. I despair. Why put any dog through this sort of trauma? Trimming dogs is not a battle of strength or wits. If this lady had been a hairdresser and the dog a child, would she have still fought hand and fist with him?

Most dogs are far more ready to please you than children are. If you tie them up by neck and stomach, put a muzzle on them and fight them until they're subservient, what can you expect other than trouble?

This inexperienced person should have left the ears alone, and a vet or more experienced groomer should have been sought for consultation.

CLIPPER PHOBIAS

Electric clippers are greatly feared by some dogs. Why is it that a dog that is pleased to see you will sit on a table and be brushed, yet, the minute the clippers are turned on, it leaps six feet in the air?

Stop. Think. Why is the objection so acute?

• Does the dog have arthritis, which is fairly common, or some other bone or growth pain abnormality? If so, take this into

Elderly dogs are often clipped for their own comfort – but be aware that some golden oldies can be grouchy because of arthritis.

account when handling the dog (and check with the owner that the dog is receiving veterinary attention). For example, infected mouths with sore abscessed teeth and gums will cause some dogs to fight a clipper on their face due to pain.

• Has the dog been burned with hot clippers in the past? It is a good idea to use cool, lubricating clipper spray every five to 10 minutes to keep the blade free-running and cool. Test the blade on your own face every so often.

• Has the dog, perhaps even at the age of a few years old, never had a pair of clippers near it? If this is the case, the dog will need to be introduced to the sight, smell and sound of the clippers in a calm, controlled way. Have the clippers running nearby while brushing the dog so it gradually gets used to the sound. Only when the dog is comfortable with having the clippers nearby should you attempt to use them.

Most of the problems that occur during trimming can be attributed to lack of consideration by the owner and sometimes the groomer. Sometimes the owner causes the problem when brushing at home. Lack of

patience, physically wrestling the dog into submission, hurting the dog without realizing it – these things must be recognized and overcome.

Often, owners tell me that their dog tries to bite them when they attempt to brush it, yet this same dog is as good as gold when it comes to the parlor. It is unlikely that the dog is behaving this way because it is spoiled and belligerent, but rather because the owner inadvertently hurts the dog, scraping his skin with too severe a brush, or twisting the dog's legs into awkward positions to achieve an objective. A little know-how goes a long way.

FIRST-TIMERS

Most dogs are nervous on their first visit to a new groomer, but they soon settle down, especially when you sing along to the radio or hold a conversation with the dog or somebody else. Your calm voice and casual manner will settle a dog quicker than anything.

Dogs very easily learn to sit, stand and stay on the grooming table without the aid of contraptions. A groomer takes on, as part of the job, the responsibility to teach the dog what is required of it in a calm and caring

Talking to the dog and acting in a calm, confident manner puts most first-timers at ease.

manner, without fuss and bother (page 17). Dogs of most breeds thoroughly enjoy going to the grooming salon. If you have more than your fair share of objecting dogs, then perhaps it is time you took more training or considered another career.

As a child growing up around horses, it was impressed upon me that I could never win a physical battle with anything that was more than twice my size and strength. The way forward was training with reward for response, gaining the animal's confidence and cleverly enticing it to respond and behave in an acceptable way.

Dogs have teeth that bite. They use them when they are confused, scared or cornered. It comes back to the fact that anyone can trim the hair off a stuffed dog, but it takes a special person to become a good groomer who understands dogs.

SOCIAL SKILLS
One would never believe how much diplomacy counts in the grooming game. Dealing with dogs is much easier than coping with nervous, neurotic, uncaring, overbearing and supercilious people, but it is all part of being a dog groomer.

Thankfully, on the whole, dog owners care about their dogs (sometimes too much). Only occasionally is there a time when tempers are so frayed that the dog owner gets a good taste of the whipping edge of my tongue. Neglect is one aspect that makes me livid. There is no need for it. There are so many groomers around that there is no need to visit a groomer only once a year, or when the dog is in a disgusting state.

There are occasions when the breeder is at fault, telling the new puppy owner that the dog should not be clipped until it is 6 months old (that's the story we are frequently told); this usually ends up with the owner leaving the dog until it is a year old. By this time, the coat is looking scruffy and out of control, with accumulated mats.

THE CUSTOMER IS ALWAYS RIGHT
Groomers do, from time to time, fall out with clients, usually because of the neglect of

a dog, but sometimes because the groomer wants to trim a dog a certain way and the client prefers the dog all clipped off. It is as well to remember that the customer is always right. This may not be the case, of course, but as a groomer it is your job to give the customer what he or she wants.

Groomers that have a fetish for combing out knots and tangles and turning out a first-class trim may be admirable and deserve recognition, but sometimes it is more appropriate to opt for something simpler and easier to manage. For example, perhaps the dog leads a lifestyle whereby it is forever getting wet and muddy; perhaps the owner never puts a brush near the coat; or perhaps the owner just wants the dog to have a very short haircut for their own convenience. In such instances, there is nothing wrong with clipping the dog all over with a No. 5 Oster blade.

I know some groomers who will refuse to do this, but I don't understand why. If the dog is comfortable and the client is happy, where's the problem? The dog must come first. A matted dog is an unhappy dog. It will be much happier having its hair clipped short than enduring hours of having its mats and snarls ripped through with a brush.

NERVOUS OWNERS
Some owners are reluctant to leave their dogs. I don't see this as a problem. I invite the owner to stay and watch the proceedings, explaining that some dogs do act up with their owners present, but it won't bother me if it doesn't bother them. Once the owner is confident in your ability, they will happily leave the dog in your care.

Some owners are often shocked that I do not possess a muzzle – I never have – and I don't tie dogs to grooming contraptions or hooks on the wall. Dogs soon learn to sit or stand still and to be groomed, clipped, stripped, whatever. A little training goes a long way.

Putting people and their dogs at their ease is a gift and is incorporated into the training of any good groomer. It may take a bit longer to trim the dog this way for the first couple of visits, but the effort is worthwhile.

SECTION THREE: BREED PROFILES

The following chapters, split into coat types, give step-by-step instructions on grooming each breed of dog. Please note that, while the breed standards are touched upon, anyone wishing to know more about any particular breed is well advised to contact the relevant club or association for complete standard and comprehensive details. Contact your national kennel club for details.

The breeds are listed in alphabetical order, using their American Kennel Club names. To locate a breed according to its British Kennel Club name, refer to the index (pages 285–288) to find the correct page number.

10 CORDED AND CURLY COATS

CORDED COAT CARE

Dogs with long, corded coats are fairly rare, and are not breeds that usually frequent the grooming salon, although they are to be seen at most shows around the world in increasing numbers.

These dogs require specialist attention. The coat on corded breeds is totally unique and in other breeds would be considered as a bundle of tangles. Certainly, these dogs would be the inexperienced groomer's nightmare.

Trying to be objective about corded coats doesn't come easily to me. I have met and judged more unsavory-smelling corded dogs than clean ones. I cannot see how the dog can be happy and contented like this. Of course, there are some admirable, dedicated owners who keep these dogs in tiptop condition, and I wouldn't want to denounce them. Hopefully, as the breeds gain popularity, more attention will be paid to their coats.

Certainly, underneath the coat, most of these dogs are little charmers, although not necessarily easy living companions because of their working tendencies and the difficulty in keeping the coat.

CURLY COAT CARE

Curly coats are very attractive, and are shorter and easier to manage than the corded type. However, they still require attention and nurturing if the dog is to look good.

Tight curls are frequently rubbed and wetted, and the longer curled coat (such as the Bolognese) is combed through regularly; daily is best. If left, this type of long, curled coat will felt (just as the Poodle coat will), so the hair must be combed through from the skin down to remove all dead hairs and to prevent matting.

This procedure should start from puppyhood, continuing vigilantly through the change of coat, and into adulthood.

BERGAMASCO

COAT: The coat is the main feature of the breed, and the long mats are known as "broccoli."

The coat is abundant and long. It is harsh in texture on the front of the body, and softer on the head and limbs. There is a short dense undercoat which obscures the skin. The hair tends to form into strands or loose mats from the top of the body, rather than into cords. The coat is greasy to the touch.

The coat color is gray, solid or with white spots. Spots may be a shade of gray. Solid black is allowed, but should be dull and not at all shiny. Solid white is discouraged, but white markings are acceptable if not more than 20 percent.

MAINTENANCE: The mats are split by hand into manageable sizes while the dog is young – the coat is never brushed. The head hair can be combed. Think very seriously before taking on this responsibility.

PROCEDURE

Equipment needed: Wide-toothed comb.

Breed tip: The Bergamasco may look as if it has never received any grooming attention, but it actually requires quite intensive maintenance. It is wise to consider this before taking on the responsibility.

- Separate the mats (broccoli) by hand where required to prevent the hair from becoming one solid mass.

- If bathing is undertaken, shampoo in an easy-to-rinse natural application and rinse very thoroughly.

- Air- or cage-dry.

- Check the dog's nails, ears and teeth.

- Go through the coat to ensure the mats are well separated, and comb through the topknot with a wide-toothed comb.

- The dog is shown in a natural state. The pet dog and those that are no longer exhibited in the show ring are sometimes trimmed down to about 2 inches (5 cm) or more all over.

BERGAMASCO COAT CARE: THE EXPERT'S VIEW

The owner of the Albera Bergamasco kennel, Maria Andreoli, graduated in biological chemistry and then dedicated herself to university research. This scientific preparation was later an invaluable store of knowledge in the setting-up of the sheepdog kennels. She says that, after accurate and patient work, she was able to determine the genetic information of this breed, which had up to then been bred using disorganized and empirical methods. Here, Maria shares her expertise on effective grooming for this breed.

COAT CARE

When dealing with a Bergamasco for the first time, people are generally worried about taking care of the coat. They ask if it is true that a Bergamasco should never be brushed, and what they should do when large bunches of hair start to form.

In practice, the Bergamasco's coat needs little care, but it must be applied at the right moment. We can divide the coat care required into three periods.

FROM BIRTH TO 10 TO 12 MONTHS
During this period, the dogs have puppy coats that are soft and short. This coat shows no felting tendency, so occasional brushing with a steel-toothed brush is sufficient to keep it in order and to remove dirt among the hairs.

DURING THE SECOND YEAR OF LIFE
Around the 10th to 12th month (individual variations and seasonal variations are very common), the formation of hair with different texture begins, together with molting of the puppy hair. The first visible sign of this is that the coat seems to rise, as if it were blown up due to the growth of the fine, abundant undercoat which blends with the puppy hair that is gradually molting.

Starting at the rear of the body, on the croup and back legs, the woolly hair makes its appearance, while, first on the tail and later in

BOLOGNESE

COAT: The Bolognese has a distinctive non-shedding coat, rather like the Poodle's, which forms into flocks.

MAINTENANCE: The coat does not require trimming in the true sense, but needs care and attention, with regular combing to prevent tangles from forming. These dogs are shown in their natural state, but sometimes pet dogs are trimmed (scissored), as with the family pet Bichon Frise and Poodle. They are bathed and conditioned frequently, and sometimes put into a "lamb"-type clip (see Chapter Seventeen). Pet dogs are often trimmed with a snap-on comb for an allover uniform length (see bottom right).

PROCEDURE

Equipment needed: Wide-toothed comb.

Breed tip: Initial thorough combing will save you a lot of hard work.

- Comb the dog through from the roots to the ends with a wide-toothed comb. Then work through the coat with a medium comb to remove dead hair and tangles. All this should be done before you even start to contemplate bathing your Bolognese.

- Bathe the dog with a protein pH-balanced shampoo.

- Rinse thoroughly to ensure all traces of shampoo are removed from the flocks.

- Use a quality antimat conditioner, and rinse if the instructions advise.

- Cage- or lightly blow-dry, using a diffuser. Use your fingertips to help circulate air throughout the coat. Part any hair that may have matted onto the skin, forming a felt. This will not happen if the dog is thoroughly groomed beforehand.

- Check the dog's nails, ears and teeth.

- Check under the dog's pads, removing excess or clogged hair.

- Where the dog is trimmed down to a manageable length, use only a coarse blade (such as an Oster No. 7, or a No. 40 with $1/2$-inch/1.25-cm attachment).

Pet Bolognese are often given an allover trim.

BOLOGNESE ON THE MENU

Gina Taylor and Barbara Andrews are two devotees of the Bolognese. Here they share their expertise on this wonderful little newcomer with a big personality that is growing in popularity in North America.

GOLDEN RULES

The golden rule when grooming the Bolognese is never to bathe the dog without first giving the coat a thorough combing through, otherwise the coat will become very matted.

The dog is laid flat on its side on a table or towel spread across a lap. A long-toothed wide-spaced comb is worked through the coat, a small section at a time, and care must be taken to groom right down to the skin. The legs, feet, face and ears are groomed with a smaller shorter-toothed comb, as the hair here is shorter and of a finer texture. After thoroughly combing with a wide comb, follow with a finer comb to ensure all knots are removed. Done gently, dog and owner will enjoy the experience. The dog is now ready for bathing.

BATHING

Using a sprayer to ensure an even distribution of water, wet the dog thoroughly with warm water, and apply a shampoo especially designed for white dogs. To prevent unnecessary matting, try to keep the hand motion straight rather than rubbing in circles. Lather well, smoothing the shampoo through the coat. Rinse thoroughly and apply a conditioner to help stop the coat from knotting. After rinsing, towel-dry.

DRYING

The unique coat will now fall into very loose curls (rather like a shaggy perm). It can be left to dry naturally in a warm room or it can be lightly blow-dried using a hair-dryer with a diffuser.

WEEKLY CARE

The coat needs to be combed twice a week. Some tangles will require extra attention – a touch of hair-dressing cream can help to combat the static that causes this.

PUPPY COAT

A puppy coat needs more attention as it is of a finer texture and changes gradually to an adult coat by the time the dog is about 18 months old. The coat does not molt, but a little hair does come out each time you comb.

PET AND SHOW

No trimming is required for the show ring, but hair can be removed between the pads. Pet dogs are frequently cut down shorter.

CORDED POODLE

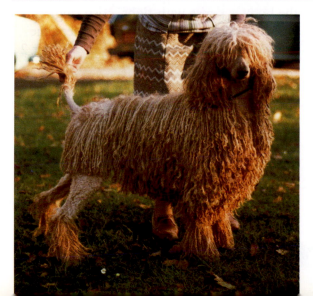

COAT: Cords can grow to an amazing length, sometimes longer than the dog.

A classic Champion from yesteryear was Champion Achilles who stood 23 inches (57.5 cm) high at the shoulder while his cords hung down for 30 inches (75 cm). He was described as a magnificent Poodle with much dignity and great carriage. His hair was never combed, but continually rolled and twisted.

KOMONDOR

COAT: The coat consists of long, coarse cords, which may be wavy or curly, with a softer undercoat. The hair tends to cling together like tassels to give the corded appearance. The color is always white, and the skin is gray, but pink skin is acceptable.

MAINTENANCE: If neglected, the coat forms into large, matted "plates." The cords are strong and heavy, and feltlike to touch. For the show ring, the Komondor is presented as corded.

PROCEDURE

Equipment needed: Scissors (to trim the adult coat, particularly the feet).

Breed tip: Do a lot of research before taking on this breed.

- Check through the cords and separate those that are matted at the skin.

- Bathe the Komondor in a shampoo, made from pure, natural, therapeutic ingredients of tea tree and lavender. When choosing a suitable shampoo, make sure it has easy-cleaning capabilities and is soothing and calming to the skin.

- Rinse the coat thoroughly, being careful that no trace of shampoo is left in, as it will be very itchy for the dog.

- Squeeze the excess water from the coat with superabsorbent towels.

- Air- or cage-dry.

- For pet (nonshow) dogs, the stomach can be clipped with Oster No. 4 for comfort and cleanliness, as can the anal area.

- Check the dog's nails, ears and teeth.

- Finish by checking all the cords to separate any clogs next to the skin.

LAGOTTO ROMAGNOLO

Photo: Kemp.

COAT: The coat of the Lagotto is its most important feature. Every part of this dog is covered with a thick, woolly-textured, double coat that forms tight, ring-shaped curls and is highly water-resistant. The coat on the head forms looser, more open curls.

LAGOTTO PUPPY COAT

From 7 weeks of age, the puppy should be groomed every few days, using a medium-toothed steel comb. Between 10 and 12 weeks, the coat on the head and body should be scissored to about 3/4 inch (2 cm) in length. The hair on the tail is trimmed to 1/2 inch (1 cm).

At 5 months of age, a Lagotto is ready for its first clipping, which is undertaken with an Oster No. 10 or No. 81/2, depending on the time of year. The development of the desirable curls can be greatly increased by frequent clipping in the first two years of a dog's life.

The color is off-white and solid; white with brown or orange markings; brown roan, brown (in different shades) with or without white; orange with or without white. Some dogs have a brown or dark brown mask. Tan coat markings (in different shades) are allowed.

MAINTENANCE: Given that the coat is nonshedding, it will, in time, felt and thus the coat must be clipped off at least once a year. The companion or working Lagotto is usually clipped two or three times a year, depending on the rate of hair growth. Show dogs are usually clipped 10 to 12 weeks before a major show and scissored between shows to maintain the outline.

Heads are not clipped, as the coat on the head is much slower-growing. Scissoring to maintain head shape is preferable.

When prepared for the show ring, the length of the coat should be about 11/2 inches (4 cm), springing back to about 3/4 inch (2 cm), and must evenly follow the line of the dog. It can be longer on the head, but must not obscure the eyes. It is permitted to remove hair in the genital/anal area.

A dog presented like a Poodle or Bichon Frise, clipped, sculptured or in any way glamorized, is highly undesirable. The correct coat presentation is functional and helps to maintain and enhance the rustic look that is typical of the breed.

The Lagotto is normally clipped using an Oster No. 10. If a midwinter clip is necessary, No. 81/2 is more suitable.

The Lagotto also requires regular bathing, particularly its beard, and must always be allowed to dry naturally.

Remember, the coat must never be brushed or combed while it is wet.

PROCEDURE

Equipment needed: Good-quality medium-toothed steel comb. Plastic or composite combs are not strong enough. A steel de-matter, good-quality slicker, and wide-blade grooming scissors are also required.

Breed tip: When grooming – whether for a show, working or companion dog – it is important that the finished dog presents a thoroughly functional, appearance. Although of small size, the Lagotto is a working dog, not a large toy dog.

Three days before the show, comb and demat the coat, bathe and dry naturally. Two days before, scissor over any loose curls to maintain the outline. The morning of the show, spray the coat lightly with water to encourage it to curl.

- Before bathing, demat the coat. If the coat is very felted, it may be necessary to first reduce the length with scissors. Lagotto coats are very water-resistant, and dogs with coats longer than 2 inches (5 cm) will be very difficult to wet to the skin. Use a natural shampoo and rinse well. Follow with a

SOFT COATED WHEATEN TERRIER

COAT: The coat, when natural, is soft and silky. It is neither woolly nor wiry, and is loosely waved or curly. If curly, the coat has large, light and loose curls. The coat should not standoff, but flow and fall naturally. The coat is abundant all over the body and equally profuse on the head and legs. The length of leg coat should be sufficient to give good balance to the length of coat on the head and body. The color is wheaten, but youngsters may have dark markings, which should clear with maturity.

MAINTENANCE: The coat is non-shedding so requires regular attention to remove dead hair and to prevent matting. Overtrimming or styling is considered wrong. For the show ring, it is permissible to tidy the coat to give a neat outline.

In Britain, this breed is shown in full coat, and in Ireland and elsewhere it is more heavily trimmed, but never to the extent of the Kerry Blue.

The Soft Coated Wheaten Terrier is a natural dog, and should appear as such. However, for the purpose of the show ring, the coat may be tidied up to present a neat outline, but the breed should not be clipped, stripped or styled.

The main differences between the U.K. and U.S. Wheatens are in the finish. The coat on the ears, for instance, may be left natural or the fringe trimmed off to accentuate their smallness, but they are not clipped so short as to appear shaved.

Secondly, thinning scissors are used to "tip" the coat (i.e., trim off the ends of the hair), as well as to thin it and to make the hair lie flat.

All trimming should create a balanced look, so that no one part of the body is accentuated.

PROCEDURE

Equipment needed: Wide-toothed comb, straight scissors and thinning scissors.

Breed tip: A wide-toothed metal comb is recommended for the Wheaten coat when it comes to daily grooming, as a slicker or pin brush tends to split the coat ends and strips out new hair growth.

- Comb through with a wide-toothed comb to remove dead hairs and to ensure no tangles are present.

- Mats and tangles can be removed by parting them with the finger and thumb, and then teasing them with the end of the comb. If necessary, use a mat-splitter – with care. Alternatively, spray the coat with conditioner to ease combing.

- Bathe the dog in a quality natural shampoo, such as tea tree and lavender.

AMERICAN METHOD

There is a great deal of variance in this breed in the United States. The Soft Coated Wheaten Terrier can look completely different on the East Coast as opposed to the West Coast. This applies to both pets and show dogs.

The pet dog is often clipped with a coarse blade or attachment blade to leave about one 1 inch (2.5 cm) of coat, or it is scissored shorter for the convenience of the owner and for the comfort of the dog.

The show dog, however, is groomed quite differently to its British show cousins – the differences are noted in the

following profile. As with any breed, you must study the breed club's recommendations and breed standard regarding coat presentation before entering any shows.

- Rinse well.

- Apply a quality conditioner to enhance the texture of the coat.

- Comb through, after thoroughly towelling the coat, and leave it to dry naturally. Or, separate the hair and gently blow-dry to assist drying. Do not overblow, as this will destroy the natural wave of the coat. Make sure you blow-dry the coat in the direction it should lie, so the coat lies nicely and doesn't appear overly fluffy.

- Comb through the coat once more with a wide-toothed comb.

- The head is trimmed with thinners from the back of the eye to the neck, and from the top of the ear to the throat, leaving the beard forward-facing, and giving the head a rectangular shape. The top of the skull is slightly domed in the U.S. ▼ 1

- Eyelashes should remain intact as these help to hold the hair away from the eyes.

- The head is not clipped short for general purposes, but this is sometimes requested by pet owners.

- The ears are trimmed to a V-shape, following the contours of the ears.

▼ 11

▼ 12

BEARDED COLLIE

COAT: The Beardie has a double coat. The undercoat is soft, furry and close-lying. The outercoat is flat, harsh, strong and shaggy, free from woolliness and curl, though a slight wave is permissible. There is long hair and a beard on the face (hence the breed's name).

MAINTENANCE: Needs constant attention to keep the coat free of tangles and looking good.

PROCEDURE

Equipment needed: A good-quality bristle brush, a pin brush, a large, wide-toothed wooden comb and a metal comb with wide teeth at one end and fine teeth at the other end.

Breed tip: A leave-in conditioner for brushing the dog when dry will make the job a little easier.

- Some people prefer to have the dog lying flat on its side when grooming; others prefer the dog to be standing. Do whatever works best for you.

- Start with the bristle brush, lifting the coat up and starting at the bottom and working through the coat in layers – this will ensure that the whole of the coat is reached. Brush in a coat-restorer or conditioner to ease the separation of the hair (use an untangle cream where necessary).

- Work through the coat again, this time using a pin brush. At this point, any mats will become apparent and can be worked on first with the brushes, then progressing to the wooden wide-toothed comb.

- A comb should only be used when the coat has been groomed with a brush first, otherwise any knots will pull a great deal and cause the dog discomfort. Do not bathe if the dog is matted – the coat must be tangle-free before you proceed.

- Bathe the Beardie in a protein pH-balanced shampoo, and use a quality conditioner.

- Blow-dry the coat, brushing continually using a pin brush. Use a lanolin lubricant to enhance texture and to prevent breaking or matting. Some people use a straightening conditioner, which is brushed or combed in after the shampoo and rinse (it should be rinsed out well). However, this is not really needed, as a Beardie coat is allowed to be wavy for the show ring – it does not need to be dead straight.

- The hair is parted along the spine by combing out the undercoat to leave it flat.

- Check the dog's nails, ears and teeth.

- In pet dogs, scissor the hair beneath the dog's feet and also under the tail (around the anus area) to prevent it becoming soiled with feces.

- Thinning scissors, or a de-matting thinner tool, can be used on an excessively profuse coat, taking care not to remove too much coat at a time.

BRIARD

COAT: The breed's flowing coat requires thorough and regular grooming, not forgetting the mustache, beard and eyebrows. The hair is about 2¾ inches (7 cm) long, slightly wavy and very dry, with a fine, dense undercoat. It is a picture to behold when given regular attention, but can look very bedraggled when neglected and left to mat and felt.

MAINTENANCE: Maintenance is fairly high as the coat will lose hairs into itself and

COTON DE TULEAR

COAT: A characteristic dry, flyaway coat, which is rather like cotton thread and is considered hypoallergenic. The hair is white (biscuit or cream included), black and white, or tricolor, and about 4 to 5 inches (10 to 12.5 cm) long. The coat is intended to protect the Coton from the equatorial sun in its native lands surrounding Tulear in Africa.

MAINTENANCE: The coat is long, dry and nearly straight, and requires brushing to remove an undercoat and to prevent matting. The Coton is a good candidate for the grooming salon, though pet dogs often have the coat cut to a more manageable length.

PROCEDURE

Equipment needed: Pin brush and a wide-toothed comb.

Breed tip: This breed can remain relatively clean without too many baths, provided the coat is groomed regularly. In addition to regular brushing at home, many owners take the dog to a professional groomer on a monthly basis.

• Brush the coat carefully. Do not bathe the dog with mats in the hair, as this will cause them to escalate.

• Bathe the dog in a natural, gentle shampoo.

• Add conditioner to aid brushing.

• Blow-dry the coat gently, brushing with a pin brush, and taking the hair away from the heat. Dry in small sections to prevent matting.

• If the dog is not being shown in the ring, it helps to mist the coat with a leave-in spray conditioner as you brush and dry.

• Check the Coton's nails, ears and teeth.

• Check underneath the dog's feet and between the pads for clogged hair, and remove with scissors, if necessary.

• Brush over the coat, using a fine grooming spray if required.

HAVANESE

Photo: Alan Walker

COAT: The coat is soft and silky, wavy or slightly curled. The Havanese is full-coated with an undercoat. Any color (or color combination) is acceptable.

MAINTENANCE: The coat is not trimmed

for normal purposes or for the show ring, but regular brushing is required. Some pet dogs are either clipped or scissored down to a manageable length.

PROCEDURE

Equipment needed: Pin brush, and a wide-toothed comb. A slicker brush can be used on tough tangles, but otherwise avoid a slicker – it is generally too harsh.

Breed tip: It is important that a loose, natural look is achieved in this breed.

- Brush through the entire coat, removing any tangles, and then comb with a wide-toothed comb.

- Bathe the dog in a natural or protein shampoo.

- Rinse the long coat well.

- Apply a conditioner to enhance the coat texture and to aid grooming.

- Blow-dry gently with a pin brush, making sure you go away from the skin.

- Check the dog's nails, ears and teeth.

- Check the feet for hair that may have clogged between the pads, and remove if necessary.

- Brush along the back. The dog will generally shake the hair so it falls naturally in a parting. Do not use a comb to achieve a perfectly straight parting.

- The topknot can be tied up away from the eyes (but not in the show ring).

JAPANESE CHIN

COAT: The coat is profuse, long, soft, straight, of silky texture and absolutely free of curl or wave. Not too flat, it has a tendency to stand out, especially at the frill of the neck. The profuse coat is colored either black and white, or red and white.

MAINTENANCE: The coat sheds and mats, so regular brushing is required to remove dead hairs that will otherwise mat.

PROCEDURE

Equipment needed: Pin brush and a wide-toothed comb.

Breed tip: Enhance the coat with an occasional boost from a quality coat spray.

- Brush through with a pin brush then work

through with a wide-toothed comb.

- Bathe the dog in a tea tree and lavender or protein shampoo, making sure you rinse away the shampoo completely.

- Use a conditioner to enhance the coat quality.

- Blow-dry gently, brushing the coat away from the heat.

- Check the dog's nails, ears and teeth.

- Check under the feet for matted hair and trim away if necessary.

- Brush the coat once more. Start along the spine, and brush outwards from there.

- Keep the face clean!

LHASA APSO

COAT: This jaunty and proud little dog is an impressive sight when in full show coat, set off with a beautifully plumed tail. The coat is long, heavy, straight and hard, neither woolly nor silky. The undercoat is moderate. This breed has a parting down the middle.

MAINTENANCE: Grooming is required on a regular basis to keep the coat free from tangles and mats. The hair on the head falls down the sides of the face, but is usually tied up when not being shown.

PROCEDURE

Equipment needed: Pin brush, bristle brush and a wide-toothed comb.

Breed tip: Pets are frequently clipped short all over with a No. 4 or No. 5 Oster blade.

- Brush through the coat with a pin brush.

- Then comb with a wide-toothed comb, using a groom spray if necessary to remove tangles.

- Bathe the dog in a protein or suitable shampoo.

- Rinse thoroughly, and apply a quality conditioner to enhance the coat.

- Blow-dry the coat in sections with a pin brush.

- Check the dog's nails, ears and teeth.

- Lightly spray with a coat conditioner and brush with a bristle brush.

- Create a straight, precise parting down the back and brush the coat down either side.

LHASA FEVER

Sally Pointon has had a lifelong interest in dogs, and has been involved with Lhasa Apsos for more than 20 years.

DAILY CARE

According to Sally, getting the Lhasa in peak condition involves day-to-day care, both

Sally Pointon and Ch. Chethang Emogene at Ballito.

mentally and physically. The coat, although an obvious part of the finished show dog, is just the icing on the cake, albeit an important one.

START EARLY

Start by table-training the puppy from day one of its coming into your care, and you will find that, by the time it needs daily care, the pup will be well behaved and accustomed to the methods you adopt. Remember, you can only obtain the best from the coat it was born with – for even the best coat care cannot make a poor coat into a good one.

NURTURING HEADFALL

To achieve a good headfall, start with banding a single topknot when the coat starts to flop over the eyes (at about 3 to 4 months), making sure that it does not pull. The band should always be cut out carefully to prevent damage and loss of hair. Once the hair gets too full or heavy, two bunches can be used (one each side), and eventually four (two each side). Face bands are also a good idea once the whiskers start getting long enough to get tangled up in the mouth.

FOOT CARE

Trimming out the hair between the pads (using a fairly blunt, small pair of scissors) is undertaken from an early age; and if you want your Lhasa to lie down quietly while you groom, this should be attempted slowly and when the puppy is feeling confident on the table, at around 3 to 5 months, depending on its temperament.

A pair of sharp, slightly curved scissors will achieve the best results on the feet and for the desired coat length; do this about a week before a show to give a neat but natural appearance.

WEEKLY BATH

Bathing and blow-drying once a week often produces better results than daily brushing – however, brushing out any obvious mats using a detangling spray may be necessary between bathing, saving time and coat in the long run.

Pulling knots apart by thumb and finger will help to separate the hair, but this should only be done if absolutely necessary. Knots often come out more easily on a wet coat during blow-drying. Brushing a dry coat can break the length or cause split ends.

Thorough rinsing after shampooing is essential, and using an absorbent towel or synthetic chamois to squeeze the excess water will cut down on drying time.

A brush should only be used initially, brushing the coat in layers from the skin to the end of the hair until the coat is tangle-free and dry. Use a pin brush and a bristle brush, choosing one of the many on the market to suit you, and depending on the coat texture. The wide-toothed steel comb is used for the whiskers and finishing off.

REGULAR REGIME

The key to achieving the best results is to work out a regime to suit the coat, and to stick to it, no matter how tired or busy you might be. Beautiful coats presented to perfection are not achieved the night before a show – they take hours of dedication throughout the year.

MALTESE

COAT: The coat is of good length, straight, silky, never woolly or crimped, and without an undercoat. It is always pure white, but slight lemon markings are permissible. The tail is well feathered.

MAINTENANCE: This breed needs a lot of attention to keep the long, silky coat in perfect order. The hair is parted along the middle from the skull to the tail and needs constant grooming. The topknot is tied back in one or two bows.

Sometimes these dogs come into the grooming parlor matted from top to bottom where the owners have frequently bathed them and left them to dry without brushing and combing out the tangles. In such cases, the only option is a short-back-and-sides clip all over.

Many pet owners have this breed clipped down to about 1 inch (2.5 cm) all over; use an Oster No. 5 to trim the hair before the bath. Condition, blow-dry and neaten any stray hairs with scissors. If clipped, this dog should look sweet and pretty – but still needs grooming.

PROCEDURE

Equipment needed: A pin brush, a bristle brush, a wide-toothed comb and an eye comb.

Breed tip: Use a light spray of water or grooming spray on the coat to aid daily brushing and to prevent breaking the hair.

• Brush through the entire coat using a pin brush.

• Spray in a little conditioning spray to aid grooming.

• Comb with a medium- or wide-toothed comb (depending on the thickness of the coat), and an eye comb. Always remember to do this before you bathe the dog, or matting will occur.

• Bathe the Maltese in a protein, pH-balanced or natural shampoo, ensuring that you rinse thoroughly.

• Apply conditioner and work through the coat. Again, rinse well.

• Next, blow-dry the coat, brushing the hair with a pin brush away from the skin (do not put the blower on the skin).

• Check the dog's nails, ears and teeth.

• Finish with a light spray of grooming conditioner, and groom in with a bristle brush.

OLD ENGLISH SHEEPDOG

COAT: The coat is of good, harsh texture, not straight, but shaggy and free from curl. The undercoat is of waterproof pile.

MAINTENANCE: The Old English Sheepdog needs a great deal of attention to keep its profuse coat even half-decent.

In ordinary circumstances, the coat is not scissored or clipped, but pet owners and breeders of retired show dogs frequently have the coat clipped to a more manageable length.

Dogs need regular attention and should be professionally or expertly groomed every four to six weeks.

PROCEDURE

Equipment needed: Slicker or pin brush, and a wide-toothed comb.

Breed tip: It is essential to keep on top of the grooming to prevent the coat from becoming one solid mat.

• Brush through the entire coat with a slicker or pin brush, working in sections from the back foot upward. Where excessive matting is present, use a mat-splitter to break through the matted felts.

• Comb with a wide-toothed comb.

• Bathe in a suitable tea tree and lavender shampoo (or similar), being vigilant about rinsing.

• White-enhancing shampoo can be used on the coat for that extra sparkle. It can also be used on the beard where saliva stains have formed (whitening cream washes are available from pet stores and grooming outlets).

• Apply a coat-enhancing conditioner.

• Blow-dry, lifting the hair with a pin brush. This separates the sections, avoiding tangles.

• Check the dog's nails, ears and teeth.

• Check under the feet for matted hair and remove carefully with scissors.

PET CLIP

With the pet dog, it is often required or requested that the entire coat of the adult Old English Sheepdog be cut off to about 2 inches (5 cm) in length. This can be done with scissors after bathing and drying is complete, or by clipping the dog, before bathing, with an Oster No. 40 with a ³/₄-inch (2 cm) attachment.

Some owners want the body hair left on, but are keen to have the hair thinned, and the coat clipped from underneath (stomach, under the arms and inside the groin area) for hygiene reasons and to keep the dog smelling sweet.

PEKINGESE

COAT: The Peke's coat is long and straight, and has a profuse mane extending beyond its shoulders, which forms a cape around the neck. The top coat is coarse, with a thick undercoat. Feathering on the ears is profuse, as on the legs and tail. All colors and markings are permissible.

MAINTENANCE: Brushing regularly is essential. On pet dogs, it is often as well to clip underneath the stomach and upward to the chest, as well as around the genital area. This will not be seen unless the dog rolls over on its back, and will aid comfort, keeping it cooler and cleaner. Do not do this to show dogs, however.

PROCEDURE

Equipment needed: Slicker or pin brush, and a wide-toothed comb.

Breed tip: Wrinkles and folds in the skin must receive regular attention.

- Brush through the entire coat, removing any tangles that may have formed, particularly underneath, with a slicker or a pin brush. Then work through the coat with a wide-toothed comb.

- Bathe in a natural-ingredient shampoo, being vigilant about rinsing. Use a facecloth on the head, rather than spraying it with water.

- Blow-dry the hair in sections.

- Check the Peke's nails, ears and teeth.

- Also check under its feet for matted hair, and remove it with scissors.

- Clean the dog's eyes gently with a damp pad or cloth, and be sure that the folds or wrinkles on the face are free from moisture, drying this area carefully with cotton pads if necessary.

- Treat the coat with a coat dressing and brush over to finish. The coat is brushed away from the parting along the back.

POLISH LOWLAND SHEEPDOG

COAT: The coat of the Polish Lowland is long, dense, shaggy, thick and of harsh texture with a soft undercoat. Long hair covers the eyes. A slight wave in the coat is permissible. All colors are acceptable.

MAINTENANCE: Needs regular brushing at least three times a week.

PROCEDURE

Equipment needed: A slicker or pin brush, and a wide-toothed comb.

Breed tip: Not unlike the Bearded Collie (page 90), the Polish Lowland Sheepdog needs considerable coat care. Lift the hair, and brush and comb it in sections to remove all tangles.

- Brush through the coat using a slicker or pin brush, and comb through with a wide-toothed comb.

- Bathe in a natural shampoo to prevent the coat from drying. Rinse thoroughly.

- Apply a conditioner. Rub in well, and rinse.

- Comb again with a wide-toothed comb. Add a light spray of conditioning oil if required.

- Check the dog's nails, ears and teeth.

- Pet dogs can have their hair trimmed from underneath and between the pads.

- Note: the pet dog is sometimes trimmed to about 2 inches (5 cm) all over with an Oster No. 30/40 with a $^3/_4$-inch (2 cm) attachment.

SHIH TZU

COAT: The chrysanthemum look of the Shih Tzu's head is most attractive and is accentuated by the hair growing upwards on the bridge of the nose. The coat is long, dense, not curly, with a good undercoat. A slight wave is permitted.

MAINTENANCE: The hair on the head is tied up to keep it away from the eyes. This coat requires regular brushing, and some pet owners have this breed trimmed down to a manageable length of about 4 inches (10 cm).

PROCEDURE

Equipment needed: Pin brush and a wide-toothed comb.

Breed tip: Pet dogs are often seen clipped all over with a No. 4 or No. 5 Oster (No. 7 blades are usually used for matted dogs). The head is either trimmed shorter with scissors or clipped to the same length as the body, according to the owner's wishes and his or her capability to maintain the coat.

- Brush through the entire coat, removing dead hair.

- Comb with a wide-toothed comb, applying a spray of grooming conditioner where necessary.

- Bathe the dog in a suitable shampoo, rinse well and apply a coat-nourishing conditioner.

- Blow the hair dry, brushing with a pin brush in small sections.

- Check the dog's nails, ears and teeth.

- Check beneath the feet for matted hair and remove with scissors.

- Check any wrinkles or folds on the face.

Clean them with a damp pad and thoroughly dry with cotton-wool (cotton) pads.

- Lightly spray with a finishing conditioner, and brush through with a bristle brush.

- The hair is parted and brushed away from the spine.

- The plumed tail hangs over the back to one side and is thoroughly brushed along with the entire coat.

SKYE TERRIER

COAT: The coat is long, profuse and glamorous. The undercoat is short, close, soft and woolly. The outercoat is long, hard, straight, flat and free from curl. The hair on the head is shorter and softer, and veils the forehead and eyes. The majority have pricked ears, but drop ears that lie flat are permissible.

The color is black, gray, fawn or cream with black points.

MAINTENANCE Coat needs regular weekly (or more frequent) brushing and combing.

PROCEDURE

Equipment needed: Pin brush, wide-toothed comb.

Breed tip: Prevent tangles by pressing the coat dry with a towel, rather than rubbing it.

- Brush the entire coat with a pin brush.

- Comb through with a wide-toothed comb.

- Bathe the dog in a natural-ingredient shampoo, using conditioner to enhance coat texture. Rinse thoroughly after each application.

- Towel off the excess water, without rubbing, to prevent the hair from tangling.

- Finish off the drying with a blower, while brushing lightly with a pin brush.

- Brush over the coat, parting the hair along the middle of the back to fall gracefully down the sides.

- Check the dog's nails, ears and teeth.

- This breed is often clipped all over with a No. 5 Oster if the dog is not exhibited, or if it has retired from the show ring.

TIBETAN TERRIER

COAT: The Tibetan Terrier has a double coat, consisting of undercoat and topcoat. The undercoat is fine and woolly. The topcoat is profuse and fine, but not silky nor woolly; it is long, either straight or waved, but never curled.

MAINTENANCE: This dog needs regular brushing and combing to keep it looking smart. Pet owners frequently have the coat trimmed back into the manageable length it was in puppyhood.

PROCEDURE

Equipment needed: Pin brush or slicker, and a wide-toothed comb.

Breed tip: When brushing the coat, lift and separate it in sections, and use a water or grooming spray to aid the removal of dead hair.

- Brush through the coat with a slicker, starting at the bottom of the back foot and working up in sections to remove dead and matting hair.

- For neglected coats, a mat-breaker will be required to slice through the felts.

- Work through the coat with a wide-toothed comb.

- Regularly bathe the Tibetan Terrier in a protein or suitable shampoo.

- Rinse thoroughly to remove all the shampoo and apply a quality conditioner to enhance the coat and to help prevent further tangles from forming.

- Blow-dry the hair in sections, brushing through with a pin brush.

- Check the Tibetan Terrier's nails, ears and teeth.

- Check under the feet, removing mats and excess hair with scissors, if necessary. However, leave the hair between the pads, because the hair here acts as protection for the pads.

- The coat is groomed away from the parting on the spine and the tail comes forward over the back.

- A pet dog can have its stomach, underarms and inside-thighs clipped with a No. 5 or No. 10 Oster, and the hair is trimmed around the anal area.

- The Tibetan Terrier often comes into the salon with a request from owners to clip the entire coat off to a length of about 1 inch (2.5 cm).

YORKSHIRE TERRIER

COAT: The coat on the Yorkie's body is said to be moderately long, but it is often seen hanging down to the ground in show dogs. It is perfectly straight (not wavy) and glossy, and has a fine, silky texture. The fall on the head is long, colored a rich golden tan.

MAINTENANCE: The glory of this dog in full coat is spectacular. A great deal of time and expertise is required to keep the coat of this tiny but hardy dog in such splendor. Often this breed is seen in the grooming parlor clipped down to about 1 inch (2.5 cm) all over because the owner really cannot cope with all the hair dragging on the ground.

PROCEDURE

Equipment needed: A stiff bristle brush and wide- to medium-toothed comb. Pet coats that are thick and woolly may require a pin brush. A slicker brush should never be used.

Breed tip: Keeping the dog in long coat is a full-time occupation.

- Brush through and remove all mats with a mat-breaker and a mat-removing anti-tangle cream, if required.

- Bathe the dog in a suitable shampoo for skin and coat quality. Apply a conditioner or balsam dematting conditioner to enhance the coat.

- Blow the hair dry, brushing continuously with a pin brush.

- Check the Yorkie's nails, ears and teeth.

- Spray with a conditioner, and brush through with a bristle brush.

- Where pet owners wish to have the hair clipped from this breed, and most do, clip off all over with a No. 5 or No. 7 blade before the bath. Or clip the body and leave the trousers like those seen on the "Lamb" clip of the Poodle (see Chapter Seventeen). The face is clipped or scissored to 1 inch (2.5 cm), leaving whiskers if desired. Many pet owners like their Yorkies trimmed like a Schnauzer.

- The show dog will have constant care applied to the coat, and wrappers or "crackers" will be placed around small sections of the hair, all over the dog, to prevent the hair from breaking, and to help it to grow to a glamorous length.

12 *MEDIUM-LENGTH COATED BREEDS*

MEDIUM-LENGTH COATED BREEDS IN THIS SECTION:

SHETLAND SHEEPDOG
- Australian Shepherd
- Australian Terrier
- Belgian Sheepdog and Belgian Tervuren
- Bernese Mountain Dog
- Border Collie
- Borzoi
- Cavalier King Charles Spaniel
- Chihuahua (Long Coat)
- Clumber Spaniel
- Dachshund (Longhaired)
- English Setter
- English Toy Spaniel (King Charles)
- Flat-Coated Retriever
- Glen of Imaal Terrier
- Golden Retriever
- Gordon Setter
- Grand Basset Griffon Vendéen
- Irish Red and White Setter
- Irish Setter
- Irish Wolfhound
- Kooikerhondje
- Large Munsterlander
- Nova Scotia Duck Tolling Retriever
- Otterhound
- Papillon
- Petit Basset Griffon Vendéen
- Pyrenean Sheepdog
- Saluki
- Scottish Deerhound
- Silky Terrier (Australian)
- Spinone Italiano (Italian Spinone)
- Sussex Spaniel
- Tibetan Spaniel
- Welsh Springer Spaniel

COAT CARE

Dogs that have this type of coat are usually attractive, elegant, even stunning looking when the hair is brushed and nurtured. They are relatively easy to work on, but still require regular attention if they are to be kept at their best.

Most of these breeds frequent the grooming parlor. For the groomer, these breeds are a joy to work on and look splendid when finished as a show dog or pet. Beautiful dogs deserve beautiful care.

The breeds in this category rarely mat, but some of the more active, working types collect burrs and other debris, which have to be removed. Odd bits of trimming are executed on some breeds (such as the Golden Retriever's tail), and thinning scissors are also used.

SILKY SMOOTH

This category contains several different coat types, such as harsh-coated breeds (e.g., Australian Terrier) and silky-coated breeds (e.g., Papillon).

Those breeds that do require a silky coat will need special consideration given during bathing and conditioning to use the correct preparation for the texture of the coat. Of course, conditioners and other coat softeners should be avoided for harsh-coated breeds.

SHETLAND SHEEPDOG

Featured is the Shetland Sheepdog Felthorn Holly Hobby, owned by Barbara Thornley.

COAT: A sturdy little dog with a double coat, the soft undercoat and harsh outercoat make the Sheltie able to withstand the winter elements. The mane and frill are very abundant, and the forelegs well feathered. The hindlegs above the hocks are profusely covered with hair; it is smooth below the hocks and on the face.

MAINTENANCE: Fairly straightforward. Simply requires a weekly brush, although more frequent brushing will be needed when the coat sheds. Do remember: frequent brushing gives you the opportunity to keep a close eye on your dog's skin condition.

PROCEDURE

Equipment needed: A nylon or nylon-and-bristle brush on a rubber cushion. A medium-toothed comb is needed for the front legs, behind the ears, and the hocks.

Breed tip: This breed likes to be on the go, so talk to the Sheltie when you groom it to keep it occupied.

- Brush the entire coat with a pin brush, removing the dead coat without stripping out the undercoat. 1

- Comb the coat through with a wide-toothed comb.

- If the hair is tangled and difficult, spray it with a grooming conditioner. Thick, neglected dense undercoat can be broken with the mat-splitter without ruining the coat too much, and it is better for coming out. The brushing/combing procedure of removing old coat can be arduous for dogs that do not have regular attention, and the mat-breaker may be required to strip some of this coat out. 2

- Bathe the Sheltie in protein pH-balanced shampoo or natural-ingredient shampoo, such as tea tree and lavender oil. 3 4

- Rinse thoroughly. 5

- Apply conditioner. Alternatively, use a purifying shampoo and mask as a toning treatment for the skin, and also to nourish the hair, three times a year.

4 ▶

- Dry with a power blower after absorbing as much moisture as possible by towel-drying the coat. 6

- Brush the dog throughout the drying process with the pin brush. 7

- Comb with a wide-toothed comb. 8

- Check the dog's nails 9, ears 10 and teeth. 11

- Scissor-trim the Sheltie's hocks to a neat appearance. 12

5 ▶

- Trim under the pads, between the toes (only removing the tufts which stick up by using the scissor-points) 13, and around the foot to neaten to an oval shape. 14

- The finished dog. 15

6 ▼

7 ▶

8 ▶

for show purposes, and is thoroughly brushed, combed and conditioned. The pet dog is frequently clipped all over with a No. 7 blade, and sometimes clipped on the body with the trousers left on the legs, which are blended in with scissors.

PROCEDURE

Equipment needed: Bristle brush.

Breed tip: The Australian Terrier's coat will tangle underneath if it is not combed at least once or twice a week.

- Brush with a bristle brush, using a spray conditioner where the coat is dry (to prevent breaking).

- Comb with a wide-toothed metal comb.

- Bathe the dog in a pH-balanced shampoo and rinse well.

- Dry with a blower, or use a cage-dryer.

- Check the dog's nails, ears and teeth.

- Trim the hair out from under the feet.

- Strip out loose hair from the body with your finger and thumb, or a stripping knife, and blend straggly hair with scissors, leaving feathering on the back of legs.

- The tail is trimmed to neaten the outline.

- Neaten the dog's feet.

- Some people express a wish to have the hair clipped off to 1 inch (2.5 cm) in length all over. Those pets with body hair left can have their stomach and anal area clipped with an Oster No. 10 blade for hygienic convenience, or trimmed with scissors.

- Use thinning scissors from the dog's hock to the foot to give an even appearance.

- Clip or strip the back of the ears to a neat appearance.

BELGIAN SHEEPDOG AND BELGIAN TERVUREN

Belgian Sheepdog

Belgian Tervuren

COAT: The Belgian Sheepdog is longhaired with a harsh-textured black coat; the Belgian Tervuren has the same coloring as the Belgian Malinois (see page 153), but the outer coat is long, straight and abundant.

All varieties (Belgian Sheepdog, Belgian Malinois, Belgian Tervuren and Laekenois – see also page 153) have double-textured coats, with a harsh outercoat and a dense undercoat.

MAINTENANCE: Requires regular brushing at least once a week. Mature males tend to molt with the weather, but bitches lose their coats very dramatically about three months after they have been in season. They are likely to look quite dreadful at this point! The coat then takes about two months to grow back.

Puppies have a much thicker, bigger coat than adults, which they lose when they are about a year old.

PROCEDURE

Equipment needed: Slicker brush and a good-quality comb.

Breed tip: This is an active, working breed that will need regular brushing to remove from the coat any debris acquired after their energetic walks.

- Use a slicker to brush through the coat, after spraying lightly with a conditioner to protect the hair and to encourage growth. The coat should always be brushed when damp, not when dry. Misting with water is fine if no conditioner is available, and indeed is the correct thing to use for show preparation (as water is the only substance that is permitted).

- The coat should be brushed up the wrong way and then brushed right down to the roots with the slicker. Work in sections to take the coat back the right way again.

- Pay particular attention to the trousers and ruff. Long hairs here and on the undercarriage can get very matted between the back legs.

- Where the undercoat needs removing, use a rake or a twisting-teeth comb.

- If the dog is in molt, use a molting comb to remove all dead hairs.

- If the dog is neutered, the coat needs a lot more attention as the undercoat can become very dense and clumped. Daily attention is needed for spayed bitches and castrated dogs, using a twisting-teeth comb, particularly on the rump, flanks and back legs. Light trimming of the very long, wispy hairs that can grow in the neutered coat makes the dog much smarter-looking and more comfortable.

- Obviously, the Belgian Sheepdog and Belgian Tervuren coats, being longer, need more attention than those of the shorthaired Belgian Malinois or the rough-coated Laekenois (see page 153).

- Bathing these dogs is rarely necessary. If the dog is muddy, remove the worst with a bucket of cold water and a sponge (outside is best for this) or use a garden hose set at a gentle pressure. Dry the dog with an old towel and then, when it is nearly completely dry, gently brush out any remaining mud. The coat readily loses mud by using this method.

- Check the dog's nails, ears and teeth.

- Next, investigate under the dog's feet. If necessary, scissor out any excess hair and any build-up of debris.

- Finish with a light application of coat-enhancing spray.

- Note: the show dog may need a few days for the coat to settle after bathing.

BERNESE MOUNTAIN DOG

COAT: Of medium length, silky with a natural sheen and a fine undercoat. The coat should not curl, but may be slightly wavy.

MAINTENANCE: In general, brushing is required once or twice weekly after a major groom and bath – more if the coat is shedding. Bitches usually cast their coats twice a year; males cast once a year.

The Bernese is a naturally presented breed, apart from trimming around the outline of the feet and underneath the feet, as well as tidying the hair on the back pastern.

PROCEDURE

Equipment needed: Slicker or hard bristle brush, both a medium- and a wide-toothed steel comb, and round-ended scissors.

Breed tip: If mats have formed behind the ears, mane, tail, breeching and feathering, dab a drop of baby oil on the mat, work the oil into it, and then gently divide the mat into pieces and use the wide-toothed comb to break it up. Work in from the outside of the mat. Do take care not to pull on the dog's skin while doing this.

• A light spray of conditioner will aid brushing.

• Work from the head to the tail in small overlapping areas. Brush the outer hair first, then comb the same area to separate the hair to the skin, taking care not to scratch the skin and ensuring that all tangles are removed.

• Next, bathe the dog in warm water, using a good, low-lather shampoo. Be sure to rinse well. Let the dog shake itself before toweling, and comb the coat again before drying.

• Check the dog's nails, ears and teeth. Nails are not usually a problem in the breed, but, if dewclaws are present, these should be kept trimmed.

BORDER COLLIE

COAT: The Collie has two varieties of coat – moderately long, or smooth. The topcoat is dense and medium-textured, while the undercoat is soft and dense. In the longer variety, the abundant coat forms a mane, breeching and brush.

MAINTENANCE: Fairly easy, simply requiring a weekly brush.

PROCEDURE

Equipment needed: Soft slicker, and a medium-toothed comb.

Breed tip: The Border Collie coat looks easy to maintain – provided it is groomed regularly. Some coats can be quite profuse, and will mat terribly if neglected, so a groom at least once a week is vital.

- Brush through the coat with a soft slicker.

- Comb with a medium-toothed comb, removing any tangles and dead coat with the help of a dematter if necessary.

- Make sure you check the breeching and behind the ears for mats.

- Bathe the Collie in a protein shampoo, being careful to rinse thoroughly.

- Use a purifying shampoo and mask (used together) about three times a year, to nourish and enhance the coat and skin.

- Blow-dry or cage-dry the coat.

- Check the Collie's nails, ears and teeth.

- Scissor the hair to a tidy and smooth appearance from the back of the hock to the foot. This can be done to the show dog, as well as to the pet dog, as long as the trimming is not excessive.

- Scissor from the back of the pastern to the foot or front leg, to neaten the appearance.

- Finish by brushing in a light spray of coat conditioner, if required.

BORZOI

COAT: The long, silky coat has a slight wave and comes in numerous colors. Short and smooth on the head, ears and front legs, the coat is much longer on the body, with heavy feathering on the backs of the legs, the hindquarters, tail and chest. The neck carries a large, curly frill.

MAINTENANCE: Coat requires dedicated application from the groomer to prevent it from becoming tangled. These dogs look magnificent when regularly beautified.

PROCEDURE

Equipment needed: Slicker or pin brush on long hair; bristle brush on shorter hair; a comb.

Breed tip: A balsam conditioner will help to prevent static electricity in the coat.

- Thoroughly brush the entire coat with a slicker or pin brush. Remember never to use a slicker on parts that have short hair.

- Remove dead hair and mats with an untangle cream or comb, or both.

- Bathe the Borzoi in a good-quality shampoo and rinse thoroughly. Apply a balsam conditioner to enhance the coat and to lessen the effect of static electricity.

- Towel-dry or use absorbent towels to remove most of the water from the coat.

- Blow-dry while brushing the hair in the direction of its natural growth.

- The hair on the neck and top of body can be flicked forward to allow the blower to lift the hair, leaving a more accentuated topline.

- Check the dog's nails, ears and teeth.

- Trim the hair underneath and between the pads, and around the anus for good hygiene.

CAVALIER KING CHARLES SPANIEL

COAT: The coat is silky and free from curl; a slight wave is permissible. There is plenty of feathering, which should not be trimmed for the show ring.

MAINTENANCE: Although trimming is not permitted for show dogs, many pet owners like the feet to be trimmed of feathering, especially in winter. Some even advocate that all feathering is removed.

PROCEDURE

Equipment needed: Slicker brush and comb.

Breed tip: Pet or show dog, this is a delightful creature to groom.

- Brush the dog thoroughly with a slicker.

- Comb through the coat to ensure all tangles are removed, using an untangle spray if necessary.

- Bathe in a natural pH-balanced shampoo.

- About every four months, use a purifying shampoo and mask conditioner to enhance the coat and skin.

- Dry with a blower, making sure you go along with the hair growth, rather than against it. Alternatively, cage-dry after combing through the coat with a balsam conditioner.

- Check the dog's nails, ears and teeth.

- Many pet owners like the thicker-coated dogs to be thinned out. Use thinning scissors with the growth of the coat, and comb thoroughly before assessing whether more thinning is necessary.

CHIHUAHUA (LONG COAT)

COAT: The Long Coat has a soft texture, which is either flat or wavy. There is feathering on the ears, feet, legs and tail. Pants on the hindquarters and a large ruff on the neck are considered desirable. The tail should be long and full (plumed). The color is any mixture.

MAINTENANCE: Easy to maintain with weekly brushing. The Long Coat may need attention a couple of times a week.

PROCEDURE

Equipment needed: Cushioned bristle brush, medium-toothed comb.
   See page 159 for the Smooth Coat Chihuahua.

Breed tip: A companion breed, the Chi loves the attention of being groomed.

• Brush through the entire coat with a natural bristle brush and then comb to check that tangles have not formed.

• Bathe the Chihuahua in a suitable shampoo, such as natural tea tree and lavender oil. Unless they get very dirty, a bath every three months should suffice. Rinse well.

• Condition the coat with a coat-enhancing cream.

• Blow-dry the coat, brushing the long hairs.

• Next, comb through the feathers.

• Check the dog's nails (they should be moderately short), ears and teeth.

CLUMBER SPANIEL

COAT: The Clumber Spaniel's coat is an abundant one. The coat is close, silky and straight, while the legs and chest are well feathered.

MAINTENANCE: The Clumber Spaniel is a breed that requires regular weekly brushing in order to keep the coat in the best condition.

PROCEDURE

Equipment needed: Slicker brush and a comb.

Breed tip: The Clumber Spaniel's eyes can be a problem, so do not forget to check them carefully as part of your regular grooming routine.

• Brush the coat with a slicker to remove dead hair and tangles.

• Bathe the Clumber in a suitable shampoo and thoroughly rinse.

• Apply a coat conditioner.

• Dry with a blower, ensuring you work along the hair growth to encourage the coat on the body to lie close.

• Check the dog's nails, ears and teeth. It is also advisable to clean the eyes (page 59), as the breed can suffer from tear stains.

• Tidy the hair from the back of the hocks with scissors, and trim off any hair that is obvious between toes.

• It may be necessary to thin the hair under the ears to allow them to lie flat.

• Excess hair on the skull can be smoothed with thinners.

DACHSHUND (LONGHAIRED)

COAT: The Longhaired Dachshund has a soft texture with straight or slightly wavy hair. The color is variable, but dapples should be evenly marked all over, and no white is permissible. There is red, black and tan, chocolate and dapple.

MAINTENANCE: The long coat, which is ideally flat and silky, needs little attention except for a regular comb-through to keep it free from tangles, and to help remove hair which is shed during a molt.

For details of the Smooth and Wirehaired Dachshunds, see page 161.

PROCEDURE

Equipment needed: Bristle brush, medium-toothed comb.

Breed tip: These hounds love following their noses, going down holes and sniffing in the undergrowth, and always end up with a great deal of the countryside in their coat! Consequently, a quick brush at the end of every walk is advisable.

• Brush the entire coat with a pin brush or slicker.

• Check for mats by combing through the coat with a medium-toothed comb.

- Dachshunds all benefit from an occasional bath, using a good dog shampoo. Rinse thoroughly, and dry with a blower or in warm air. Bathe the dog at least several days before a show to allow enough time for the coat's natural oils to be replenished.

- Check the dog's nails. The Dachshund's nails should be regularly trimmed for show and pet dogs, and must be done with great care since the quick (the nerves and blood supply) cannot be seen.

- The ears can be wiped with cotton batting, and the teeth should be kept clean by regular brushing.

- Check under the tail and remove excess hair from around the anus.

- Add sparkle to the coat by lightly spraying (or applying with your hand) some coat-finish lanolin. Of course, if you are showing your dog, no substances must be added to the coat.

ENGLISH SETTER

COAT: The coat is basically white, either lightly or heavily flecked with blue or orange (known as "belton"). The blue or orange can be of different shadings. Occasionally, lemon or liver beltons are seen. Blue beltons with tan around the muzzle and feet are known as tricolor.

The coat from the back of the head, in line with the ears, is slightly wavy (not curly) and, like the rest of the coat generally, is long and silky. The breeches and forelegs nearly down to the feet are well feathered.

MAINTENANCE: The coat is trimmed in parts to accentuate the dog's elegance and glamor. The art of trimming an English Setter is to make a clean and tidy outline, while maintaining a natural appearance. Thinning scissors should only be used for cutting up and into the lie of coat. This will mean that it is only the undercoat that is removed, allowing the topcoat to lie flat. Scissors are not used on the back or sides of the dog as, ultimately, the coat will be ruined – often permanently.

Clippers should not be used on the body, as this will ruin the gentle, flowing look of the coat. Some Setters do have a thick and unruly coat, and the temptation is to clip this off. However, consultation with the owner is essential before performing this procedure.

PROCEDURE

Equipment needed: Slicker brush and fine-toothed comb.

Breed tip: It is advisable only to cut once or twice with the thinning scissors before brushing out the loose hair. This way, you can check if sufficient hair has been removed and will not accidentally overtrim.

Novice pet owners who decide to show their English Setters would be well advised to seek the advice of an experienced show exhibitor.

- Brush through, being careful to remove any tangles. Use untangle cream if necessary.

- Next, turn your attention to the head. The soft, tufty down that grows on the head is best removed by gently plucking with the thumb and finger, taking a little at a time.

- The neck: the hair under the neck grows in an upside-down fan shape (down to the breastbone, curving out towards the shoulder and ears). With the thinning scissors, clean out this fan-shaped area until the hair on both sides of the neck blends in with the longer hair on the shoulders.

- The ears: with the thinning scissors, cutting upwards into the long hair, repeat the cutting action until all the hair is short and lies flat. Leave the hair on the front edge of the ear longer, giving the desired soft expression. Remove the hair from under the ears so that the ears lie close to the neck.

- The tail: with the thinning scissors, remove the hair from under the base of the tail to about 1 inch (2.5 cm). Brush the tail feathers well. Then, holding the feathers firmly against the tail, measure against the top of the Setter's hock. The tail should stop at this level or slightly above. With the ordinary scissors, remove all the excess hair that falls past the end of the tail, or, if the fleshy part of the tail is short, cut a little further down. Once you let the tail-feathering loose, it will then fall in a scimitar shape.

- The back of the pastern: using the thinning scissors, trim off all the excess hair that can be found growing down the back of the hock to the foot.

- The feet: with a pair of ordinary scissors, trim off the hair around the pads. Then, with the thinning scissors, trim the excess hair from between the toes. To do this, view the foot from the top. With your thumb, pull up all the excess hair from between the toes, cutting upwards from the nail toward the leg, using several cutting motions until all the protruding hair is removed. This method is applied to both front and back feet.

- Bathe the English Setter in a suitable shampoo.

- Rinse thoroughly and then apply conditioner.

- Towel-dry the dog, then blow-dry along the growth of the hair. Alternatively, cage-dry after combing through the entire coat.

- Check the Setter's nails, ears and teeth.

ENGLISH TOY SPANIEL (KING CHARLES)

COAT: The coat is long, silky and straight. Slight waves are allowed, but the coat should never be curly. The legs, ears and tail are feathered profusely.

Colors:
- Black and tan (rich, glossy black, with bright mahogany tan markings on the muzzle, legs, chest, linings of the ears, under the tail and spots over the eyes. White patches on the chest are undesirable).
- Tricolor (ground color pearly white, with well-distributed black patches, and brilliant tan markings on the cheeks, linings of the ears, under the tail, and spots over the eyes. There is a white blaze between the eyes and up the forehead).
- Blenheim (ground color pearly white, with well-distributed chestnut-red patches. There should be a wide, clear blaze, with a "spot" in the center of the skull – a clear chestnut-red mark about 3/4 inch (2 cm) across).
- Ruby (whole-colored a rich chestnut-red. A white patch on the chest is highly undesirable).

MAINTENANCE: Fairly easy to maintain with regular brushing.

PROCEDURE

Equipment needed: A pin brush and a medium-toothed comb.

Breed tip: Brush and comb your English Toy Spaniel every day, from early puppyhood. The coat should not be trimmed – any loose hair will be brushed or combed out easily if regular grooming is carried out.

- Brush through the coat using a pin brush.

- Comb through with a medium-toothed comb, making sure all tangles are removed.

- Next, check the dog's skin. If you notice dandruff, do not dismiss it as dry skin – a small mite could be responsible, which causes the skin to scale. If so, you will need a special veterinary-prescribed shampoo.

- Now, bathe and shampoo the dog (a protein-enriched or tea tree and lavender shampoo work wonders) and rinse well.

- Apply a complementary conditioner.

- Blow-dry the hair, brushing in the direction of the hair growth, not against it.

- Check the dog's eyes. If necessary, wipe with cotton batting soaked in an eye-cleansing solution.

- Check inside the dog's ears to ensure they are clean and free of wax. If necessary, apply a light dusting of canker powder.

- Check the nails and cut if necessary. Also check under the feet, and trim out any excess hair between the pads.

purifying shampoo and mask, about three times a year.

- Towel-dry the coat and finish with a blower, going with the direction of growth.

- Check the dog's nails, ears and teeth.

- Trim any excessive hair from under the feet, around the pads, and the back of the hocks.

- Thin under the ears, if required, and carefully trim the edges of the ear, if necessary.

- This dog should look natural, but the tail is trimmed from the tip, tapering to form a plume. Place your finger and thumb at the end of the tail and cut a curve.

- Show dogs are groomed and trimmed regularly. Pet dogs need to be trimmed if the fringes get too long and bedraggled. In all dogs, really long fringes are impractical and untidy.

- Note: neutered or spayed dogs develop heavier coats and need more attention.

GORDON SETTER

COAT: The black-and-tan coat on the head, front of the legs and tips of the ears is short and fine. It is of moderate length, flat and as free as possible from curl or wave on all other parts of the body.

Feathering on the ears is long and silky. On the backs of the legs, it is long, fine, flat and straight. Fringes on the belly may extend to the chest and the throat.

MAINTENANCE: The coat is trimmed in parts to show off the dog to its best advantage. The art of trimming a Gordon Setter is to make a clean and tidy outline, while maintaining a natural appearance. Thinning scissors should only be used for cutting up and into the lie of the coat. This will mean that it is only the undercoat that is removed, allowing the topcoat to lie flat.

Clippers should not be used on the body, as this will ruin the gentle, flowing look of the coat. Some Setters do have a thick and unruly coat, and the temptation is to clip it off. However, consultation with the owner is essential before performing this procedure.

PROCEDURE

Equipment needed: Slicker or pin/bristle brush, medium-toothed comb.

Breed tip: As with all Setters, this breed benefits from regular (daily) brushing to keep its coat dust-free and looking healthy. It is advisable to cut only once or twice with the thinning scissors before brushing out the loose hair. This way, you can check if sufficient hair has been removed and will not accidentally overtrim.

- Brush through the coat with a slicker or pin/bristle brush to remove any tangles.

- Next, turn your attention to the head. The soft, tufty down which grows on the head is best removed by gently plucking with the thumb and finger, taking a little at a time.

- The neck: the hair under the neck grows in an upside-down fan shape (down to the breastbone, curving out toward the shoulder and ears). With the thinning scissors, clean out this fan-shaped area until the hair on both sides of the neck blends in with the longer hair on the shoulders.

- The ears: at the top of the ear, with thinning scissors, go under and against the lie of the coat for approximately 2 inches (5 cm), blending in to lie flat, making a smooth, flowing look. Remove the hair from under the ears so that the ears lie close to the neck. The rest of the hair on the ears remains long and silky.

- The tail: brush the tail feathers well. Then, holding the feathers firmly against the tail, measure against the top of the Setter's hock. The tail should stop at this level or slightly above. With the ordinary scissors, remove all the excess hair which falls past the end of the tail or, if the fleshy part of the tail is short, cut a little further down. Once you let the tail-

feathering loose, it will then fall in a scimitar shape. If any trimming is required to achieve this shape, this is best done with trimming scissors.

- The feet: with a pair of ordinary scissors, trim off the hair around the pads. Then, with trimming scissors, trim the excess hair from between the toes. To do this, view the foot from the top. With your thumb, pull up all the excess hair from between the toes, cutting upwards from the nail toward the leg, using several cutting motions until all the protruding hair is removed. This method is applied to both the front and back feet. On the front legs, with thinning scissors, from the back pads go up approximately 2 inches (5 cm), taking off excess hair. Finish with straight scissors for a neat appearance.

- The hocks: do not remove all hair off the back of the hocks. Thin and trim to the required shape.

- Bathe the dog in a suitable shampoo, rinsing well before applying conditioner.

- Towel-dry the dog, then blow-dry along the growth direction of the coat. Alternatively, cage-dry after combing through the entire coat with a medium-toothed comb.

- Check the dog's nails, ears and teeth.

IRISH SETTER

COAT: The hair on the head, front of legs and tips of the ears is short and fine; on all other parts of the body and legs it is of moderate length, flat and as free as possible from curl or wave.

Feathering on the ears is long and silky. On the back of the forelegs and on the hindlegs, the hair is long and fine, with a fair amount of hair on the belly, forming a fringe which may extend to the chest and throat. The feet are well feathered between the toes of this dog, though generally these are trimmed round to neaten. The tail fringe is of moderate length, decreasing as it approaches the tip or point.

MAINTENANCE: Relatively easy to keep, exercise and groom.

PROCEDURE

Equipment needed: A good-quality bristle brush, a pin brush to use where necessary, a wide-toothed metal comb and a finer comb for finishing.

Breed tip: Overtrimming will spoil the classic look, so any hairdressing must be carefully executed.

- Brush thoroughly with a good-quality bristle brush. Long hair can be tackled with a pin brush where required, to remove tangles.

- Comb with a wide-toothed metal comb to remove dead hair. A finer comb can then be used if more hair needs to be removed.

- Bathe the dog in a suitable mild shampoo.

- Use conditioner after rinsing thoroughly. A purifying shampoo and mask can be applied three times a year to enhance the skin and coat.

- The coat is blow-dried with the growth of the hair to keep it flat and sleek, rather than lifted and flyaway. This can be achieved by pointing the blower downwards over the dog. Spray conditioner will assist this process and leave the coat gleaming.

- Check the dog's nails, ears and teeth.

- Trimming to enhance a natural appearance, while emphasizing angulation and the good points of the dog, is undertaken as follows. Groomers inexperienced in this breed would be well advised to take expert advice on trimming particular dogs for the show ring, as every dog is different, and too much or too little trimming can spoil the overall picture of the dog.

- Head: excess hair is plucked out with finger and thumb to give the head a smooth finish.

- Neck: using thinning scissors, thin from the

throat to just above the breastbone, with the growth or lie of the hair. Trim from the underside of the ear to the center of the breastbone. The surrounding hair is blended with thinning scissors or shears to give a smooth, clean, natural appearance. Do not use thinning scissors across the grain of the coat, as this will leave a cutting, doorstep effect; only trim in the direction that the coat grows. The chest feathering falls from the breastbone to the fall of hair on the upper part of the front legs.

- Ears: thinning scissors are used on the inside and outside of the leathers, working downwards with the hair growth, to shorten the hair to a very neat appearance, removing the excess coat on the neck beneath the ear to blend in and flatten the coat. Trim around the leather to finish.

- Body: thoroughly comb through the body hair, working down the fringe of the chest to remove dead hairs and give a smooth, sleek appearance. First, use a medium-toothed comb and then a finer one if required.

- Front feet: the feet are trimmed underneath to remove excess hair, working an inch or so up the leg. Tidy around the toes with thinning scissors to give a neat appearance. Between the toes, it is beneficial to thin the excess hair to prevent it from becoming clogged with mud, etc.

- Back feet and hock: trim the rear feet following the same procedure as for the front ones (see above), to give a neat appearance. Comb the hair from the point of the hock upwards to the toes. Using thinning scissors in a downward action, remove the hair to give a flat, clean finish.

- Tail: this is trimmed to a moderate length, with the hair decreasing in a taper to the tip or point.

- The use of clippers may be undertaken when the coat has blown, and becomes extremely thick and unmanageable, as with a neutered pet for example. Clipping the Irish Setter should only be carried out as a very last resort.

1

IRISH WOLFHOUND

COAT: The Irish Wolfhound has a rough, harsh coat that needs brushing at least three times a week, with some finger plucking to keep the coat in good condition and keep the dog comfortable.

MAINTENANCE: It is fairly easy to look after the coat. All that is needed is a thorough weekly brush.

PROCEDURE

Equipment needed: Slicker brush, comb.

Breed tip: Invest in a bath ramp or get help to put this giant in the bath – or you will break your back!

- Aim to brush and comb daily, and you will probably do it twice weekly. Occasionally, you can use Savlon (a mild, gentle antiseptic cream) on a cloth, then brush out well. This will keep the Irish Wolfhound clean and smelling fresh.

- Monthly, or when necessary, remove any unwanted bushy or long, dead hair from the neck and under the belly. Pluck it out with your finger and thumb. Scissors can be used for around the genitals, under the tail and the feet.

- Trim the hair flat to the pads but do not remove from between the pads.

- Check the dog's nails. If they do not wear down, then, every month, cut the excess away with good nail clippers. Alternatively, use a rasp weekly, filing each nail a couple of times in turn so that they do not get hot. Keep going around until the nails are the correct length. The best time to do this is when your Irish Wolfhound is asleep after a meal. If you get it used to the procedure from a young age, the dog won't mind you doing it.

- Check the ears and clean them with an appropriate cleaner once a week. Check the teeth once a week.

- Only bathe once a year, during the summer months, on a nice, hot day outside. Use warm water and a good-quality shampoo.

- Try not to remove the natural oils from the coat, rinse well, towel-dry and then allow the coat to dry naturally. Do this in the morning, so you have the rest of the day for the coat to dry off.

- Do not use conditioners, as they will soften the coat; this is not allowed in the show ring.

- A good-quality dry shampoo brushed through the coat at about three-month intervals removes some grease and grime, and smells sweet.

KOOIKERHONDJE

COAT: The coat is medium-long, slightly waved or straight, but not curled, close-fitting and not too fine. It has a well-developed undercoat.

MAINTENANCE: Brushing is undertaken on a regular, twice-a-week basis with a bristle brush, and a comb is used for the feathering and tail hair. This is a relatively easy dog to look after and it looks lovely when well cared for.

PROCEDURE

Equipment needed: Slicker brush and comb.

Breed tip: The Kooikerhondje is jaunty and full of zest.

- Brush the entire coat thoroughly and comb through to remove dead hairs.

- Bathe in a suitable, mild shampoo and rinse well.

- Condition with coat-enhancing cream and rinse thoroughly.

- Once the dog has been rinsed, towel-dry to remove the drips.

- Finish drying the coat in warm air, or lightly blow-dry, going in the direction of the growth of the hair.

- Comb through the coat.

- Check the dog's nails, ears and teeth.

LARGE MUNSTERLANDER

COAT: The coat is long and dense, but not curly or coarse. It is well feathered on the front and hindlegs, and on the tail, more so in males than in bitches. The hair must lie short and smooth on the head.

MAINTENANCE: Requires brushing once or twice a week, particularly on the ears and feathering to remove debris picked up from walks.

PROCEDURE

Equipment needed: Bristle brush and comb.

Breed tip: Keep a close eye on the feathering, which tangles easily. Trim excess hair between the toes and on the back of the hocks.

• Brush through the coat with a bristle brush.

• Comb with a wide-toothed comb, and then a medium-toothed one, to remove dead hairs and to check for tangles, especially behind the ears and in the long feathering.

• Bathe the dog in a suitable mild or natural shampoo.

• Rinse thoroughly.

• Conditioner can be used, if required, to enhance and nourish the coat. Be sure to rinse thoroughly.

• Remove excess moisture from the coat by towel-drying.

• Finish drying the coat by putting the dog in warm air or a cage-dryer, or use a blower.

• Remember to check the dog's nails, ears and teeth.

• Check the feet, making sure you look at the area under the pads. Carefully remove any matted hair with small scissors.

• Finally, finish by combing through the coat one more time.

NOVA SCOTIA DUCK TOLLING RETRIEVER

COAT: The coat is straight and water-repellent. It is a double coat of medium length and softness, with a softer, dense undercoat.

The Nova Scotia Duck Tolling Retriever is allowed a slight wave on the back and has feathering at the throat, behind the ears and at the back of the thighs. The forelegs are moderately feathered.

Color: shades of red or orange, with lighter feathering under the tail. White marks are desirable in at least one of the following places: on the tip of the tail, the feet and chest, or as a blaze.

MAINTENANCE: Brushing on a regular basis is usually all that is required to keep this breed in tiptop condition.

PROCEDURE

Equipment needed: Bristle brush and a pin brush.

Breed tip: This breed will enjoy the personal interaction of being groomed, so set aside a couple of times a week to groom and keep it looking smart. Do note that excessive use of a brush will remove or damage the undercoat.

- Brush through the coat with a bristle or pin brush.

- Use a pin brush on the tail or feathering.

- Then brush through the coat with a pin brush on the body and on the feathering. Don't forget to brush behind the ears.

- Bathing can be undertaken, if necessary. Make sure you use a gentle shampoo so you do not remove the natural oils from the coat. Rinse thoroughly.

- Towel-dry. Tollers are practically "drip-dry" and they dry off in seconds, so any other form of drying (e.g., a cage-dryer) is not advised.

- Check the nails, ears and teeth.

OTTERHOUND

COAT: The Otterhound has an oily, rough double coat, which is dense but not wiry. The hair on the head is softer, as is the hair on the legs.

MAINTENANCE: The presentation is natural, but this is a dog that loves a bath, and it seems a shame not to oblige it.

PROCEDURE

Equipment needed: Slicker or curry brush and comb.

Breed tip: Do not use too harsh a shampoo, or you will strip the coat's natural oils and remove a characteristic feature of the breed.

- Brush the entire coat with a slicker or pin brush.

- Comb through with a wide-toothed comb to remove dead hair and any tangles that may be present.

- Bathe using a suitable mild shampoo. Apply a conditioner that suits the coat condition,

adding a teaspoonful of oil to it where necessary.

- Blow the coat dry, taking care that you follow the direction of the growth of the hair, brushing with a pin brush.

- Do not forget to check the dog's nails, ears and teeth.

- Finally, check under the foot, paying careful attention to the area between the pads. Remove any matted hair with scissors.

PAPILLON

COAT: The coat is long, fine and silky, and requires regular brushing. It is abundant, flowing, but without undercoat. It falls flat on the back and sides with a profuse frill on the chest. It is short and close on the skull, muzzle and front legs. The rear of the forelegs to the pasterns, tail and thighs are covered with long hair.

MAINTENANCE: Easy to maintain with weekly brushing.

PROCEDURE

Equipment needed: Plastic pin brush or bristle brush, comb.

Breed tip: A special whitening shampoo will make the coat shine.

- Brush through with a pin brush, then comb with a medium-toothed comb to ensure the coat is free from tangles.

- Bathe in a pH-balanced shampoo.

- Use white-enhancing shampoo on the white

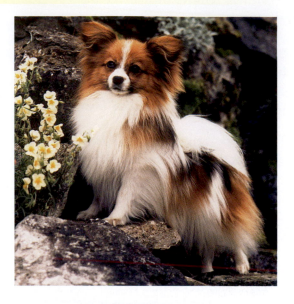

parts for that extra-special glow.

- Apply conditioner to the coat.

- Towel- and blow-dry the coat.

- Check the dog's nails, ears and teeth. The teeth need cleaning once a week, as the breed is susceptible to dental problems.

- Check under the feet. Remove any excess hair.

PETIT BASSET GRIFFON VENDÉEN

COAT: The coat is rough, long without exaggeration and harsh to the touch. It has a thick undercoat and should be neither silky nor woolly.
   The color is white with any combination of lemon, orange, tricolor or grizzle markings.

MAINTENANCE: The coat is not trimmed but needs regular grooming, brushing and combing to remove dirt and dead or matted hair, with some tidying around the head and feet.

PROCEDURE

Equipment needed: Pin or slicker brush, wide-toothed comb and a stripping knife.

Breed tip: This dog will root through undergrowth and may collect brambles, thorns or tangles in its coat, so check it over regularly.

• Brush or comb through the coat, removing any debris and teasing out any matted hair, especially under the body and armpits, and from the beard.

• Bathe in a natural, mild-ingredient or harsh-coat shampoo and rinse thoroughly.

• Towel-dry and finish in warm air or a cage, or with a blower.

• Brush the coat flat and strip away excess hair around the ears and feet.

• Clean and remove excess hair from the ear canal, clean the dog's teeth and check its nails (clipping or grinding them if necessary).

PYRENEAN SHEEPDOG

COAT: The coat is long, or semi-long. It is fairly harsh, dense and almost flat or slightly wavy. It is denser and more woolly on the rump and on the thighs. The hair on the muzzle is short, but it is longer on the face and cheeks. Acceptable coat colors include various shades of fawn, with or without black hairs, light to dark gray, blue merle, slate or brindle, black, or black and white. Large areas of white, black or tan are undesirable.

MAINTENANCE: Grooming entails brushing with a slicker and using a wide-toothed comb on a regular basis (once a week).

PROCEDURE

Equipment needed: Slicker brush or pin brush and a wide-toothed comb.

Breed tip: Never neglect underneath the feet – where the hair can form mats.

• Brush through the entire coat with a slicker or pin brush.

• Comb with a wide-toothed comb to remove dead hairs.

• This breed should only be bathed if it is absolutely necessary, and certainly not on a regular basis. If bathing is vital, a natural-ingredient shampoo should be used, and make sure you rinse well.

• Add conditioner to aid grooming.

• Towel-dry, patting the coat rather than rubbing it.

• Finish the drying process in warm air, a cage, or with a gentle blower.

• Check the dog's nails, ears and teeth. Also check the dewclaws and trim the rear ones if necessary to prevent them curling around.

• Check underneath the feet for excess hair or clogged hair, and remove with small scissors if necessary.

• Finally, complete by brushing the coat over with a bristle brush.

SALUKI

COAT: The coat is smooth, of silky texture, with feathering on the ears, tail, backs of the legs and between the toes. Puppies, and sometimes older dogs, may have a slight woolly feathering on the thigh and shoulder. The smooth variety has no feathering. All colors and combinations of colors are possible except for brindle.

MAINTENANCE: The main part of the coat is easy to maintain, requiring regular brushing with a bristle brush. The long hair on the ears, tail, and so on, needs regular (weekly) attention with a slicker brush to remove mats. If the Saluki is inclined to grow fluff on the flanks, it can be removed with a stripping stone.

PROCEDURE

Equipment needed: Bristle brush and slicker brush.

Breed tip: Use a snood while the dog is eating or chewing to save the long hair on the ears.

• Brush the long hair (particularly behind the ears) with a slicker brush and remove all mats.

• Brush the whole coat with a bristle brush to remove dead hairs.

• Bathe the Saluki in a good-quality shampoo and conditioner when necessary. The choice of shampoo is important, particularly on black-colored dogs, if the dog is inclined to shed dandruff.

• Dry the dog in warm air or with a gentle blower.

• Check the dog's nails, ears and teeth.

SCOTTISH DEERHOUND

COAT: The coat is shaggy, but not over-coated, and a woolly coat is considered unacceptable. The correct type of coat for this breed is thick, close-lying and harsh or crisp to the touch. The hair on the body, neck and quarters is required to be 2³/₄ inches (7 cm) to 4 inches (10 cm) long. The hair on the head, breast and belly is softer. A slight hairy fringe on the inside of the forelegs and on the hindlegs is typical.

   The color is dark blue-gray, darker and lighter grays or brindles and yellow, sandy-red or red fawns with black points.

   A white chest, white toes and a slight white tip on the stern are permissible, but the less white the better, as the Scottish Deerhound is a self-colored dog.

MAINTENANCE: The coat is relatively easy to maintain, needing merely a brush with a pin brush on a regular basis, and combing through with a wide-toothed comb to remove burrs, etc.

PROCEDURE

Equipment needed: Pin brush, comb.

Breed tip: The show dog must be bathed and groomed about a week before a show to allow the coat to settle.

- Brush through the coat with a pin brush.

- Bathe as little as possible. If the dog is very dirty and there is no avoiding it, bathe it using a suitable shampoo for coarse hair.

- Towel-dry and finish with warm air, a cage-dryer or a blower.

- Comb or brush through the coat once again.

- Check the dog's nails, ears and teeth.

- The Scottish Deerhound is presented as naturally as possible, though the ears can be trimmed to make them appear "mouselike."

SILKY TERRIER (AUSTRALIAN)

COAT: It has a glossy, silky coat. The color is blue and tan, gray-blue and tan; the richer these colors, the better.

MAINTENANCE: The coat is easy to look after with daily brushing with a pin brush.

Where the owner neglects this duty, tangles need to be groomed out, sometimes with the aid of a conditioning spray or a mat-breaker. Commence at the tip of the hair, working gradually toward the root. Only attempt a small amount at a time and hold the hair to prevent it being pulled and hurting the dog.

PROCEDURE

Equipment needed: Pin brush, a wide-toothed metal comb and a pure bristle brush to finish and to aid shine.

Breed tip: Brush and comb through on a regular basis, but don't get carried away or you may break the hair unnecessarily.

• Brush through the coat with a pin brush or slicker, then comb with a wide-toothed metal comb, paying attention to behind the ears and beard, as well as under the legs and belly.

• Bathe the dog in a protein or mild shampoo, rinsing well.

• Apply a good anti-tangle conditioner and comb through.

• After rinsing, pat dry with an absorbent towel and dry the hair in layers with a gentle blow from your hairdryer.

• Check nails, ears and teeth weekly.

• The hair is parted down the back, so finish off with a light brushing away from the spine, using a bristle brush.

SPINONE ITALIANO (ITALIAN SPINONE)

COAT: The coat is tough, thick, slightly wiry and close fitting with no undercoat. It is about 1½ to 2 inches (4 to 6 cm) on the body, shorter on the nasal bridge, ears and head. It is even shorter on the front of the legs and feet. The eyebrows consist of longer, stiffer hair. Even longer, softer hairs cover the cheeks and upper lips, forming a mustache and beard.

The color is white; white with orange or brown markings; white speckled with orange (orange roan) with or without orange markings; white speckled with brown (brown roan) with or without brown markings.

MAINTENANCE: This is not a glamorous breed. The Spinone Italiano is a rustic, functional dog and part of its attraction is its slightly disheveled look. Care must be taken not to overpresent this breed. Too frequent bathing softens the coat, and show dogs are best hosed down and dried naturally. Regular brushing with a slicker will remove burrs and seeds. A comb should be used on the head.

Beards need constant attention and regular washing. These dogs are very prone to ear infections – therefore, ears should be checked every day and cleaned twice a week. Hair inside the ear should be removed with a finger and thumb. Ear powder will help.

A Spinone Italiano born with the unique and very desirable "pigskin-like" skin will have the correct single coat, which needs little stripping other than to enhance the shape of the head. However, many dogs are born with longer, softer coats, and regular stripping will help to improve the coat and encourage a harsher texture.

Strictly speaking, this task is undertaken by hand, although most owners use a stripping comb (a Mars 99 M328 is excellent). A stripping block is useful for finishing and removing stray hairs.

Dogs born with soft double coats always have thin skin and these coats are almost impossible to strip. Rather than cause the dog distress, it is better to bathe and clip it.

PROCEDURE

Equipment needed: Slicker brush, bristle brush and comb.

Breed tip: Strip the coat out several weeks before a show, paying particular attention to the head and legs. Brush the body coat regularly as the coat grows in. Heads may be tidied a couple of days before a show.

- Comb with a medium-toothed comb. Comb through beard and mustache to ensure no mats or debris are present.

- Body: Strip the body and legs before the head. When stripping for the show ring, the golden rule is to strip the side nearest the cause too many problems, as only light stripping or thinning is required. The look should appear natural, and only tufts of hair are removed, as with the Springer.

PROCEDURE

Equipment needed: Pin brush or slicker, and a medium-toothed comb.

Breed tip: Use a pin brush on the long hair, and a bristle brush on the short, body hair.

- Groom the coat with a pin, slicker or bristle brush, according to coat length (see above).

- Comb through to remove dead hair.

- Use thinning scissors to shorten the hair below the hock joint.

- Next, tidy the feet to a firm catlike appearance.

- Thin out any excessive hair on the dog's head to give a smooth appearance.

- Use thinning scissors to tidy any areas that look overdressed. It is vital that the dog appear trimmed, but has a natural look.

- Bathe the dog in a suitable shampoo (tea tree and lavender, or similar).

- Rinse thoroughly.

- Next, towel-dry the dog. Then, finish in warm air or a cage, or lightly blow-dry with the coat growth.

- Check the dog's nails, ears and teeth.

13 SHORTHAIRED BREEDS

SHORTHAIRED BREEDS FEATURED IN THIS SECTION:

GREYHOUND
- Affenpinscher
- Australian Cattle Dog
- Basenji
- Basset Fauve de Bretagne
- Basset Hound
- Beagle
- Beauceron
- Belgian Malinois and Laekenois
- Bloodhound
- Boston Terrier
- Boxer
- Bracco Italiano
- Bulldog
- Bullmastiff
- Bull Terrier
- Chesapeake Bay Retriever
- Chihuahua (Smooth Coat)
- Chinese Shar-Pei
- Collie (Smooth)
- Dachshund (Smooth and Wirehaired)
- Dalmatian
- Doberman Pinscher
- Foxhound (American and English)
- French Bulldog

- German Shorthaired Pointer
- Great Dane
- Hamiltonstövare
- Ibizan Hound
- Italian Greyhound
- Labrador
- Lancashire Heeler
- Manchester Terrier
- Manchester Terrier (Toy)
- Mastiff
- Miniature Pinscher
- Neapolitan Mastiff
- Pharaoh Hound
- Pointer
- Pug
- Rhodesian Ridgeback
- Rottweiler
- Sloughi
- Staffordshire Bull Terrier
- Swedish Vallhund
- Vizsla
- Weimaraner
- Welsh Corgi (Cardigan and Pembroke)
- Whippet

COAT CARE

One would think that this type of coat is the easiest to maintain. This is not necessarily true. Because the breeds molt, they must be groomed on a regular basis – otherwise their hair will get everywhere. Short, harsh, sticky hairs attach themselves to carpets, clothes, car seats, and so on, and are extremely obstinate about being dislodged.

The answer, or at least a great help in preventing this nuisance, is to brush regularly with a sisal or hound glove. You should also bathe the dog at hair-shedding time and remove much of the offending matter by scrubbing the jacket with the hound glove while the dog is in the bath.

As with all trimmed breeds, it is advisable to check whether the dog is going to be shown before tidying any hairs you may consider straggly, as the relevant breed standard may require it to be left natural. To keep a shorthaired dog looking fabulous, breeders run a stripping knife over the coat on a daily basis, and bathe them regularly. They usually allow a few days to pass before showing them to give time for the hair to settle.

GREYHOUND

Featured as an example for this group is the Greyhound Champion Porcelain of Springflite, owned by Martin Butler and Kevin Dodd.

COAT: The coat is fine and close. This breed comes in virtually every color of black, white, red, fawn, fallow, brindle or any of these colors broken with white.

MAINTENANCE: The coat is easy to maintain with a bristle brush and hound glove. It benefits from an occasional dust-over with chamois cloth.

PROCEDURE

Equipment needed: Hound glove, bristle brush, fine-toothed comb.

Breed tip: Brush with a hound glove while the coat is still wet to remove molting hairs more efficiently.

• The coat benefits from a thorough grooming with a hound glove to remove dead hair and to stimulate healthy growth. 1

• Bathe the dog in a 2 suitable shampoo, and rub the coat vigorously with the hound glove to remove molting and dead hair while the dog is in the bath. This will save a lot of molting hair from coming out onto the furniture later.

• Remove excess moisture with an absorbent towel 3, then finish off the drying process in warm air. 4

- Check the dog's nails [5], ears [6] and teeth. [7]

- Finally, lightly spray the coat with a finishing conditioner [8] and brush the dog with a polishing silky duster or pure bristle brush.

- The finished dog. [9]

PROCEDURE

Equipment needed: Hound glove, bristle brush, fine-toothed comb.

Breed tip: Use a hound glove after bathing to remove loose hair.

- Brush the coat with a bristle brush, or lightly work through the coat with the hound glove to remove dead hair and to stimulate the skin.

- When required, bathe the Beagle in a suitable shampoo, using a superwhitening shampoo on white areas for extra brilliance.

- The body can be vigorously rubbed with the hound glove while in the bath to remove molting hairs.

- Use conditioner where required to heighten color and give a healthy gleam.

- Cage- or blow-dry after absorbing most of the moisture with a towel. Do not allow the dog to get cold.

- Check nails, ears and teeth weekly.

- Finally, brush all over with a hound glove or chamois cloth.

BEAUCERON

COAT: It comes in black and tan markings, or in a harlequin pattern where the base color is gray with black and rust torn patches.

MAINTENANCE: The Beauceron's coat is relatively easy to maintain, with regular brushing enhancing the natural, healthy appearance.

PROCEDURE

Equipment needed: Slicker brush, medium-toothed comb.

Breed tip: Brushing from an early age is essential to get the Beauceron acclimatized to handling.

- Brush through the coat thoroughly with a slicker brush to remove dead hair.

- Bathe in a natural coat-enhancing shampoo and rinse well.

- Towel-dry and finish with warm air, or a light blower.

- Check the dog's nails, ears and teeth, particularly the double hind dewclaws.

- Brush over with a hound glove or a cloth.

Belgian Malinois

Laekenois

BELGIAN MALINOIS AND LAEKENOIS

COAT: The Laekenois has a short, wiry coat; the Belgian Malinois coat is short with a firm texture. All varieties (see pages 110–111 for Belgian Sheepdog and Belgian Tervuren) have double-textured coats, with a harsh outer coat and a dense undercoat.

MAINTENANCE: Requires brushing at least once a week. Mature males tend to molt with the weather, but bitches lose their coats very dramatically about three months after their season. Regrowth takes about two months. Puppies have a thicker, bigger coat than adults; they lose it at about a year old.

PROCEDURE

Equipment needed: Slicker brush and a good-quality comb.

Breed tip: Needs regular brushing to remove any postwalk debris.

- Use a slicker to brush through the coat, after spraying lightly with a conditioner to protect the hair and to encourage growth. The coat should always be brushed when damp, not when dry. Misting with water is fine if no conditioner is available, and indeed is the correct thing to use for show preparation (as water is the only substance that is permitted).

- The coat should be brushed up the wrong way and then brushed right down to the roots with the slicker. Work in sections to take the coat back the right way again, paying particular attention to the trousers.

- Where the undercoat needs removing, use a rake or a twisting-teeth comb.

- Use a molting comb to remove dead hairs.

- If the dog is neutered, the coat needs a lot more attention. Daily attention is needed for neutered dogs, using a twisting-teeth comb, particularly on the rump, flanks and back legs.

- Bathing is rarely necessary. If the dog is muddy, remove the worst with a bucket of cold water and a sponge or a garden hose set at a gentle pressure. Dry the dog with an old towel and then, when nearly completely dry, gently brush out any remaining mud. The coat readily loses mud by using this method.

- Check the dog's nails, ears and teeth.

- If necessary, scissor out any excess hair and any build-up of debris under the dog's feet.

- Apply a light application of coat-enhancer.

- Note: the show dog may need a few days for the coat to settle after bathing.

153

BRACCO ITALIANO

COAT: The coat is glossy, fine, dense and short. The color is a most attractive orange and white, orange roan, chestnut and white, or chestnut roan. The only solid color allowed is white. The size is up to 26 inches (65 cm).

MAINTENANCE: The coat is easy to clean.

PROCEDURE

Equipment needed: Hound glove, bristle brush, fine-toothed comb.

Breed tip: Don't bathe too frequently, or you can ruin the glossy coat.

- Brush regularly with a bristle brush and hound glove.

- Not regularly bathed, a natural shampoo should be used. Make sure you rinse well.

- Towel-dry the coat, and finish with warm air.

- Brush over the coat with a glove or a cloth.

- Check the dog's nails, ears and teeth.

BULLDOG

COAT: The coat is of fine texture, short, close and smooth, not wiry.
  The Bulldog comes in various colors, including whole or smut (whole color with black muzzle) brindle; red in various shades; fawn; and fallow.

MAINTENANCE: The Bulldog is a breed that is easy to maintain with a bristle brush and hound glove.

PROCEDURE

Equipment needed: You will need a hound glove, a bristle brush and a fine-toothed comb.

Breed tip: Don't be fooled by their looks – the majority of Bulldogs are incredibly friendly, lovely dogs.

• Brush with a bristle brush or a hound glove, or both.

• Bathe the Bulldog in a protein shampoo, being careful to clean and then thoroughly dry the folds of the skin around the face, the legs and the body.

• Rinse thoroughly.

• Check the dog's feet for sores.

• Use a hound glove while the dog is still in the bath to remove dead hairs.

• Blow- or cage-dry.

• Powder the folds of the skin.

• Check the nails, ears and teeth.

• Brush a light spray of coat-enhancing or protein conditioner into the coat.

BULLMASTIFF

COAT: The Bullmastiff coat is short, hard and weather-resistant, lying flat to the body.

The Bullmastiff colors include any shade of brindle, fawn or red, and the color is pure and clear.

In accordance with the breed standard, a slight white marking on the chest is permissible but not desirable. The characteristic black muzzle, however, is essential.

MAINTENANCE: The Bullmastiff coat is generally easy to maintain.

However, as always with shorthaired breeds, the Bullmastiff will benefit from brushing and an occasional good bath – if you can get the dog in it!

PROCEDURE

Equipment needed: Hound glove, bristle brush, fine-toothed comb.

Breed tip: Start the grooming routine early, while the dog is still a puppy. An adult Bullmastiff unused to grooming can become too big and difficult to handle.

• Brush the coat very vigorously with a bristle brush or hound glove.

• Bathe in a suitable natural-ingredient shampoo, rinsing well.

• Towel-dry, and then dry the dog with warm air, in a cage-dryer or with a blow-dryer for a few minutes.

• Don't forget to check the Bullmastiff's nails, ears and teeth.

CHINESE SHAR-PEI

COAT: The coat is extremely harsh, straight and offstanding on the body, but flatter on the limbs. There is no undercoat. The length varies from short and bristly (under ¹/₂ inch/ 1.25 cm) to longer and thicker (¹/₂ inch to 1 inch/1.25 to 2.5 cm), but still offstanding and harsh to the touch.

All solid colors (except white) are acceptable. Frequently shaded with lighter color on the tail and backs of the thighs.

MAINTENANCE: No trimming is required and bathe infrequently. Care must be taken with the ears and nails.

PROCEDURE

Equipment needed: Rubber grooming mitt, stripping comb (e.g., Mars 628), large nail file.

Breed tip: Hot-spots on the coat can be treated with "flowers of sulfur" powder.

- Brush the coat with a rubber grooming mitt to remove dead hair, especially during molt.

- Bathe infrequently with a suitable shampoo.

- Rinse carefully, making sure that all the shampoo has been removed from the folds or wrinkles.

- Towel-dry.

- Check the dog's nails, teeth and ears (avoid probing too deeply with cotton swabs).

- Check the folds and wrinkled skin to ensure they are dry.

COLLIE (SMOOTH)

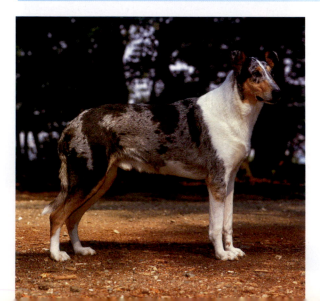

COAT: The Smooth Collie's short outercoat is water-resistant and the dense, warmer undercoat makes it totally weatherproof.

The color in this breed is frequently seen as blue merle, as opposed to the other two more frequently seen colors of the Rough Collie, which are sable and white, and tricolor.

MAINTENANCE: The Smooth Collie will easily be looked after with the minimum of fuss, only requiring a rub-down with a damp chamois cloth to turn it back into a clean, comfortable pet, even after a run in the muddiest weather. A weekly groom with a Mason Pearson type of bristle brush will remove all hair and debris, and the Smooth, which is noted for its fastidious cleanliness, will do the rest.

The Collie's coat casts twice a year and a firm daily brushing at this time is essential for two to three weeks to remove all the dead hair.

PROCEDURE

Equipment needed: Bristle brush, medium-toothed comb, natural shampoo and a complementary conditioner.

Breed tip: Trimming is not required, but the area under the feet may need attention. Trim away the long hair to prevent a buildup of debris, which will otherwise cause discomfort when it walks.

- Brush through the coat with a bristle brush to remove dead hair. Comb through with a medium- or fine-toothed comb.

- Bathe in a natural-ingredient shampoo and apply a good-quality conditioner for a sumptuous finish.

- A purifying mask and conditioner can be used on certain occasions to enhance the coat condition.

- Dry the coat with an absorbent towel and finish in warm air.

- Check the dog's nails. If necessary, the Smooth Collie's nails can be filed with a large workshop file.

- Also check the dog's ears and teeth.

- Brush over the coat once again with a bristle brush and a cloth.

- Check under the feet and remove any excess hair with scissors.

DACHSHUND (SMOOTH AND WIREHAIRED)

◄ *Smooth Dachshund*

Wirehaired Dachshund ►

COAT: Smooth: dense, short coat. Wirehaired: short, straight, harsh hair, with a dense undercoat, bearded chin and bushy eyebrows. The color is variable, but dapples should be evenly marked all over, and no white is permissible. There is red, black and tan, chocolate, and dapple. See page 116 for details of the Longhaired Dachshund.

MAINTENANCE: The Smooth coat needs no maintenance other than a brush with a soft-bristled brush and a polish with a chamois cloth.

The Wirehaired variety is generally stripped twice a year. The wire coat consists of three types:

- The ideal pin-wire coat consists of a harsh topcoat with a soft, dense undercoat. It appears so flat that, from a distance, the dog has the appearance of a Smooth Dachshund, apart from some harsh whiskers and bushy eyebrows. This coat needs little attention, other than perhaps some tidying and thinning out on the neck with finger and thumb or by using a stripping knife about two weeks before a show.

- The more usual type of wire coat also consists of a double layer, but the top hair is more profuse and there will also be more beard, eyebrows and leg furnishings. This type of coat will need stripping with a stripping knife probably twice a year to keep it tidy, and certainly quite a lot of preparation and maintenance for show condition to give the desired smooth outline.

    At least a month before a show, the hair on the neck, chest and back should be stripped right down, using a stripping knife, but only experience can be the guide to the time it takes for the new hair to grow through.

The hair under the dog must be tidy and the hair on the head should be neat and flat. Any long hair under the eyes and ears should be removed. The beard should be combed forward, and the hair behind it stripped flat. It is safer to use finger and thumb on the head area. Long hairs under the tail should be removed and just enough left at the end to cover the tip to a neat point. The hair around the Dachshund's feet should be trimmed, and the hair from the front of the forelegs should be removed. Strip away all the hair from the hocks to give a good, clean shape to the hindlegs.

- The softcoated Dachshund can be kept tidy only by stripping. Unfortunately, however, it can never be disguised. The hair on the legs, head and ears is always soft, and the harsh, even coat of the correct wirecoated Dachshund is completely lacking.

PROCEDURE

Equipment needed: Bristle brush, medium-toothed comb, stripping knife.

Breed tip: These hounds love following their noses, going down holes and sniffing in the undergrowth, and always end up with a great deal of the countryside in their coat! A quick brush at the end of every walk is highly recommended.

- Brush through the entire coat. A bristle brush or a sisal brush is the best choice for use on the Smooth and Wirehaired coat.

- Using finger and thumb, strip the Wire when required.

- Check for mats by combing through the coat with a medium-toothed comb.

- Dachshunds all benefit from an occasional bath, using a good dog shampoo. Rinse thoroughly, and dry with a blower or in warm air. For the Wirehaired coat, bathe the dog at least a week before a show, and several days beforehand for the Smooth, to allow enough time for the coat's natural oils to be replenished.

- Check the Dachshund's nails. Nails should be regularly trimmed for both show and pet dogs, and this must be done with great care since the quick (the nerves and blood supply) cannot be seen.

- The ears can be wiped with cotton batting, and the teeth should be kept clean by regular brushing.

- Add sparkle to the dog's coat by lightly spraying (or applying with your hand) some coat-finish lanolin. Of course, if you are showing your dog, no substances can be added to the coat.

DALMATIAN

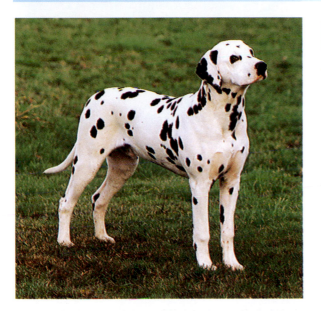

COAT: The coat is short, hard, dense and glossy in appearance.

MAINTENANCE: The Dalmatian's coat benefits from regular grooming, as plenty of hair comes out during molting periods. I once had a car that previously belonged to the owner of a Dalmatian. I had it two years and never did get rid of all the hairs stuck in the rear carpets (and it wasn't from lack of trying)!

PROCEDURE

Equipment needed: Hound glove, bristle brush.

Breed tip: When the Dalmatian is being bathed, rub the go vigorously to remove dead and molting hairs, which like to stick everywhere.

- Bathe the Dalmatian in a suitable natural shampoo.

- Rinse thoroughly, ensuring all the suds are removed.

- Rub vigorously with a rubber brush or hound glove while the dog is in the bath, to remove dead or molting hairs.

- Towel-dry the coat.

- Check the dog's nails, ears and teeth.

- Brush with a hound glove or natural bristle brush, and go over the coat one final time with a chamois cloth.

GERMAN SHORTHAIRED POINTER

COAT: The German Shorthaired Pointer's coat is short and thick. It is somewhat longer on the underside of the tail and the back edges of the haunches, and softer, thinner and shorter on the ears and head. Some pet dogs have a longer coat, but this is not desirable in the show ring.

MAINTENANCE: Maintenance is easy with regular brushing with a bristle brush or a hound glove.

PROCEDURE

Equipment needed: Bristle brush, hound glove.

Breed tip: Using the hound glove while the dog's coat is still wet will remove excess shedding hair.

- Brush through the entire coat with a bristle brush or hound glove to remove dead hairs and dust.

- Bathe the dog in a purifying shampoo, followed by a suitable mask or conditioner to enhance the coat's sheen, and rinse thoroughly.

- Vigorously use a hound glove while the coat is still wet to remove excess molting hair.

- Dry with absorbent towels, and finish in a cage or with a blower.

- Check the dog's nails, ears and teeth.

- Go over the coat one last time with a cloth or a bristle brush.

GREAT DANE

COAT: The coat is short, dense and sleek-looking, never inclined to roughness. The colors include the following:
- Brindle: a striped coat. The ground-color from the lightest buff to the deepest orange, the stripes are always black.
- Fawn: various shades from lightest buff to deepest orange, dark shading on head and ears acceptable
- Blue: varying in shade from light gray to

deep slate. The nose may be blue.
- Black: obviously, all black.
- Harlequin: a pure white underground, with (preferably) all black or all blue patches, having the appearance of being torn.

MAINTENANCE: Easy and clean by habit and the short coat is easy to maintain.

PROCEDURE

Equipment needed: Hound glove, bristle brush, fine-toothed comb.

Breed tip: Unless your bath is at ground level or you can walk the dog in along a ramp, you will need help to lift it in.

- Brush the dog with a bristle brush or a hound glove.

- Bathe in a suitable shampoo, making sure the coat is rinsed thoroughly.

- Towel-dry and finish in warm air.

- Check the nails, ears and teeth.

HAMILTONSTÖVARE

COAT: The Hamiltonstövare is double-coated. The undercoat is short, close and soft, and is especially thick during winter. The upper coat is strongly weather-resistant and lies close to the body.

This dog is richly colored in black, tan and white.

MAINTENANCE: This is an easy breed to maintain.

PROCEDURE

Equipment needed: Hound glove, bristle brush, fine-toothed comb.

Breed tip: Use the hound glove in a vigorous round action to remove dead or molting hairs.

- Brush through the coat with a bristle brush or a hound glove.

- Bathe the dog in a natural, mild shampoo when necessary.

- Rinse thoroughly.

- Remove excess moisture from the coat with an absorbent towel.

- Finish the drying process by putting the dog in warm air or a cage-dryer, or use a blower.

- Check the dog's nails, ears and teeth regularly.

LANCASHIRE HEELER

COAT: The coat is short, and consists of a fine undercoat covered by a short, thick, hard, flat topcoat. The topcoat is slightly longer on the neck. The undercoat should not show through the topcoat nor allow any longer hair at the mane to stand off. The mane may be noticeable in the winter.

MAINTENANCE: The coat is easy to maintain, requiring little more than a chamois cloth and a quick brush.

PROCEDURE

Equipment needed: Bristle brush, medium-toothed comb.

Breed tip: Polish with a cloth for the show ring to enhance the natural gleam of the coat.

- Brush the entire coat with a bristle brush.

- Comb through with a medium- to fine-toothed comb to remove dead hairs.

- Bathe the dog in a natural-ingredient shampoo, such as tea tree and lavender oil.

- Towel-dry and finish with warm air, cage or gentle blower.

- Check the nails, ears and teeth.

- Brush over with a bristle brush and chamois cloth to finish.

MANCHESTER TERRIER

COAT: It has a short, close, smooth, glossy coat of firm texture. The color is jet black and rich mahogany tan.

MAINTENANCE: Easy.

PROCEDURE

Equipment needed: Hound glove and a bristle brush.

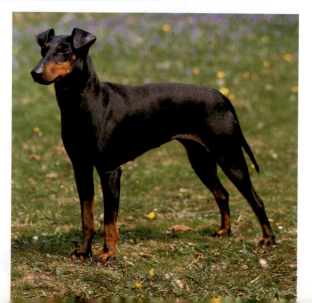

Breed tip: The Manchester Terrier's smooth, glossy coat will benefit from a polish with a cloth.

- Brush through the coat with a hound glove or bristle brush.

- Bathe in a natural shampoo to enhance the coat gleam.

- Rinse well.

- Towel-dry and finish by leaving the dog in warm air or a cage-dryer, or gently blow-dry.

- Check the nails, ears and teeth.

- Brush over and use a cloth or a velvet pad to enhance the quality of the finish.

MANCHESTER TERRIER (TOY)

COAT: Known as the English Toy Terrier in the U.K., this breed has a short, glossy coat and is well balanced, elegant and compact, sleek and cleanly built.

The coat is thick and glossy, with a density of short hair required.

MAINTENANCE: Regular brushing with a hound glove and bristle brush will keep the coat in tip-top condition.

PROCEDURE

Equipment needed: Hound glove, bristle brush, fine-toothed comb.

Breed tip: Use the hound glove while the Manchester Toy Terrier is still wet. This will help to remove excess dead hair.

- Brush through the entire coat with a hound glove.

- Bathe the dog in a natural shampoo.

- Rinse thoroughly, ensuring you have removed all the suds.

- When the dog is molting, a hound glove can be used in the bath to remove any excess dead hair.

- Use conditioner, if required, to enhance the shine.

- Towel-dry, and finish in warm air, a cage or with a light blow.

- Don't forget to check the dog's nails, ears and teeth.

- Finally, brush over the coat once again with a bristle brush, a hound glove or with velvet cloths.

- Lightly spray the coat with conditioner to enhance the gleam.

- Check the dog's teeth, brushing them if necessary.

- Check wrinkles and folds of the to ensure they are free from moisture, or they could develop eczema or sores.

- The Neapolitan Mastiff's eyes should be bathed as often as possible.

- The ears should be cleaned inside weekly or as part of the grooming routine so as to avoid recurring problems.

- Clean under the dog's chin regularly, as food collects in this area very quickly.

PHAROAH HOUND

COAT: A striking feature of the breed is its shiny, glossy coat. Hair ranges from fine and close to slightly harsh, with no feathering. The coat is tan or rich tan in color. White is allowed on the chest (the "star") and the toes, and a slim white blaze down the center line of the face is also permissible. A white tip to the tail is highly desirable.

MAINTENANCE: Easy.

PROCEDURE

Equipment needed: Bristle hound glove, rubber grooming mitt and chamois cloth.

Breed tip: Dry the dog quickly after a bath, as it really dislikes the cold.

- Brush through the entire coat with a bristle hound glove.

- Bathe in a natural ingredient shampoo with conditioner, removing dead hair with the rubber mitt.

- Rinse thoroughly, ensuring all soap is removed.

- Remove excess moisture with towels, and then leave to dry naturally – preferably in front of a warm fire.

- Check the nails. The Pharaohs' nails grow at a remarkable rate, so they need checking on a weekly basis.

- Gently clean the ears with cotton batting. Do not insert cotton swabs into the ear canal, as these can damage the Pharoah's sensitive ears.

- Next, check the teeth.

- Finally, go over the coat with a chamois cloth to provide that extra show shine.

POINTER

COAT: The smooth, hard coat should have a definite sheen, and is fine and short. It should be evenly distributed over the body and perfectly straight.

MAINTENANCE: Easy with regular brushing with a bristle brush or hound glove.

PROCEDURE

Equipment needed: Bristle brush, hound glove.

Breed tip: Using the hound glove while the coat is still wet will remove excess shedding hair.

- Brush through the entire coat with a bristle brush or hound glove to remove dead hairs and dust.

- Bathe the Pointer in a natural, purifying shampoo and mask/conditioner to enhance the coat's sheen.

- Vigorously use a hound glove while the coat is still wet to remove excess molting hair.

- Remove excess moisture with absorbent towels.

- Finish the drying process in a cage or with a blower.

- Check the dog's nails, ears and teeth.

- Go over the coat one last time with a cloth or a bristle brush.

PUG

COAT: The coat is fine, smooth, soft, short and glossy, neither harsh nor woolly. The colors are fawn or black. Fawn Pugs have a clear contrast of black masks, ears and facial wrinkles. The nails should be black.

MAINTENANCE: Easy to maintain, as it only needs regular brushing. The Pug's overnose wrinkle and ears should be checked daily and kept spotlessly clean. If a sore should develop, a vet should be consulted. Special care should be taken with the breed's eyes. They should be kept clear, and a vet should treat any damage to the eye immediately. The older Pug's eyes are particularly vulnerable, and occasionally require eye drops.

PROCEDURE

Equipment needed: A suitable brush or a grooming glove. A selection of combs is useful.

Breed tip: Watch for any sores in the facial folds.

- Brush the coat daily.

- Bathe in a suitable natural-ingredient shampoo and rinse thoroughly.

- Make sure that the Pug is completely dried.

- Check the dog's nails, ears and teeth.

- Check that any wrinkles on the face are clean and dry, wiping with cotton batting if necessary.

RHODESIAN RIDGEBACK

COAT: The Rhodesian Ridgeback's coat is short, dense, sleek and glossy, never woolly nor silky. The color is light-wheaten to red-wheaten.

MAINTENANCE: The Rhodesian Ridgeback only requires regular brushing with a bristle brush or a hound glove.

PROCEDURE

Equipment needed: Bristle brush or hound glove.

Breed tip: A hound glove or cloth will produce a sleek appearance at the end of the grooming session.

- Brush over the body with a bristle brush or hound glove.

- This breed of dog requires bathing very rarely. When bathing is necessary, use a suitable natural, mild shampoo.

- Ensure that all evidence of the shampoo is rinsed well from the coat.

- Towel-dry the coat and finish with warm air, a cage-dryer or a blower.

- Check the dog's nails, ears and teeth.

ROTTWEILER

COAT: The Rottweiler has a shiny double coat, which consists of a topcoat and an undercoat.

The topcoat is of medium length, coarse and flat. The undercoat is essential on the neck and thighs but should not show through the topcoat. The hair is also permitted to be a little longer on the back of forelegs and the breeching.

The color is black with clearly defined markings of rich tan to mahogany – a spot over each eye, on the cheeks, as a strip around each side of the muzzle (but not on the bridge of the nose), on the throat, two triangles on either side of breastbone, on the forelegs from the carpus to the toes, on the inside of the rear legs from the hock to the toes (but not completely eliminating black from the back of the legs), and on the undertail.

MAINTENANCE: The Rottweiler is easy to maintain, although regular brushing will be required at least three days a week to keep the coat at its best.

PROCEDURE

Equipment needed: Bristle brush, hound glove, fine-toothed comb.

Breed tip: If the dog is being shown, bathe it a couple of days before the show to allow the coat to settle, as the coat should not be soft.

- Brush with a hound glove or a bristle brush, or both, against the lie of the coat, (i.e., the wrong way) in order to remove loose and dead hair. Then brush back the correct way to induce polish. Finish with a comb to encourage

the coat to lie flat and to remove surface hair.

- Bathe the dog with a pH-balanced natural shampoo and use purifying shampoo and a mask a couple of times a year. Or use a shampoo especially for black- or wirecoated breeds. Alternatively, walk the dog in the rain then finish off with a dry, rough towel. This works wonders!

- Make sure you rinse thoroughly.

- Use a hound glove when the dog is in the bath to help remove loose, molting hairs.

- Towel- or cage-dry.

- Check the Rottie's nails and keep them short.

- Check the dog's ears and teeth.

- Go over the coat with a velvet pad or a silk cloth after using a spray conditioner very lightly, if required. If your dog is to be shown, conditioner should not be allowed to remain in the coat.

SLOUGHI

COAT: The coat is tough and fine. Colors include sable or fawn in all shades with or without a black mask. Also permissible is a coat that is dark, white, brindle, black with tan points, or a brindle pattern on a fawn background on the head, feet and sometimes the chest.

MAINTENANCE: Requires only regular brushing to keep clean and healthy.

PROCEDURE

Equipment needed: Hound glove, sisal brush or bristle brush, and a fine-toothed comb.

Breed tip: A hound glove is a must to remove loose hair.

- Brush with a sisal brush or a hound glove.

- Bathe the dog in a natural shampoo, and rinse.

- Dry the coat with towels and finish in warm air or a cage-dryer, or with a light blower.

- Check the dog's nails, ears and teeth.

- Go over the coat with a hound glove or a cloth for a final polish.

STAFFORDSHIRE BULL TERRIER

COAT: The coat is smooth, short, close and gleaming. It comes in a variety of colors: red, fawn, black or blue, and white. In addition, any of these colors may come with white. There is also a brindle variety, and brindle and white, which gives plenty of choice.

MAINTENANCE: The Staffordshire Bull Terrier requires no trimming, but brushing on a regular basis with a hound glove or a pure bristle brush will keep its jacket in perfect order.

PROCEDURE

Equipment needed: Hound glove, bristle brush, fine-toothed comb.

Breed tip: Most Staffords like water and enjoy a good bath – which is helpful for removing short hairs too.

• Brush through the entire coat with a hound glove.

• Bathe in a natural shampoo.

• Make sure you rinse thoroughly.

• While the dog is molting, use a hound glove when you are bathing it, and scrub thoroughly around the coat to remove any dead hairs.

• Rinse again.

• Air-, cage- or blow-dry.

• Remember to check the Stafford's nails, ears and teeth.

SWEDISH VALLHUND

COAT: The coat is harsh, close-fitting, of medium length, with a tight topcoat and an abundant, soft, woolly undercoat. The color is steel-gray, grayish yellow and reddish brown, with darker guard hairs on the back, neck and sides of the body. Saddle markings should be present. The muzzle, throat, chest, belly, feet and hocks are usually cream in color. White can sometimes occur under the throat or around the collar (one-third white is permissible).

MAINTENANCE: Easy. The breed sheds its coat twice a year – the undercoat molts first, hence the need for a rake (below).

PROCEDURE

Equipment needed: A rake-type comb (which ensures the groomer can get down to the bottom layer of the coat), hound glove, fine-toothed comb.

Breed tip: A chamois cloth is a useful addition to its grooming bag.

• Brush through the coat with a rake-type comb and a hound glove.

• Bathe in a natural tea tree shampoo, or similar

• Towel-dry and finish in a cage or with a blower. Allow a few days for the coat to settle if the dog is about to be shown.

• Check the nails, ears and teeth.

• Finally, go over the coat with a bristle brush and a chamois cloth.

179

- Trim the tail closely to the tip, toward the head. Trim very fine in the rear, where it joins the stern. **1** **3**

- Trim the stern very closely where it joins the tail, working it heavier toward the hindlegs. **3**

- Trim the skull very closely. Trim the eyebrows evenly and closely at the outside corner of the eye, with plenty of length over the inside corner. **4**

- Trim the cheeks closely from the outside corner of the eye to the corner of the mouth. **4**

- Trim very slightly from the inside corner of the eye, downward to the corner of the mouth, to achieve the characteristic breed facial expression. **4**

- Trim the hairs on top of the muzzle from slightly between the eyebrows to the nose to give a straight line from the top of the skull. **4**

- Leave the chin whiskers, but brush them forwards. Clean under the jaw from the corner of the mouth to the back of the neck. **4**

- Clean off the ears closely inside and out, giving particular attention to the edges of the ears, which should have a clean finish. **4**

- Remember to check the Airedale's nails, ears and teeth.

- Avoid bathing unless absolutely necessary – regular brushing should keep the coat clean. If a bath cannot be avoided, wet the coat thoroughly, apply a mild shampoo and rinse thoroughly. Brush the coat through with a hound glove to remove loose hairs, and towel off excess moisture. Leave to dry naturally in a warm room.

- Pet dogs are often clipped rather than stripped and trimmed.

BORDER TERRIER

COAT: The coat is harsh and dense, with a close undercoat and thick skin.

MAINTENANCE: The coat is not clipped, but will require stripping out by hand twice a year. This will give the dog a new lease on life, as well as removing uncomfortable and itchy layers of dead coat. When the hairs start to form a natural parting and fall into clumps, the dog is ready to be stripped.

Some grooming salons do not hand-strip, but it is a pity to ruin this wonderful little dog's coat by running the clippers over it. Stripping takes time; the groomer must discuss this with the owner and charge accordingly.

PROCEDURE

Equipment needed: Stripping knife, fine-toothed comb, slicker or pin brush, scissors.

Breed tip: The coat could be rolled (page 48) on a regular basis to keep the dog looking smart throughout the year.

- Comb the dog thoroughly with a fine-toothed comb.

- Starting behind the shoulders, and working down the entire body, finger and thumb hand-stripping is the correct practice ▼ 1 . However, should a knife be used, one with a serrated edge is preferable. The coat is easier to strip when it is rubbed up the wrong way. Be sure to pull the coat in the direction of the hair growth. It should come out easily if it is ready to strip.

- Part the hair underneath the tail to remove the hair on either side. Trim with scissors around the anal area.

- Take the long hair from the skull and inside the ear. 2

- Trim the hair from under the feet and between the toes.

- Bathe the Griffon in a natural mild shampoo, and rinse well.

- Towel-dry thoroughly. Cage- or lightly blow-dry.

- Check the dog's nails, ears and teeth.

- Note: For the pet, a complete strip twice a year is fine with a little tidying in between.

- The show strip is ideally done in stages – side of body and legs first, then back, then head, as they grow in different stages.

- The pet dog can be trimmed lightly with a coarse blade if required, rather than hand-stripped.

CAIRN TERRIER

COAT: The Cairn has a weather-resistant double coat. The outercoat is profuse, harsh, but not coarse; the undercoat is short, soft and close.

The color is cream, wheaten, red, gray or nearly black. Brindling in all these colors is acceptable.

MAINTENANCE: The Cairn is usually hand- or knife-stripped; pet dogs are sometimes clipped to give a cleaner, smarter appearance, but it ruins the coat, as the undercoat and topcoat are then the same length and the coat becomes quite soft.

PROCEDURE

Equipment needed: Clipping/stripping materials, scissors, stiff bristle brush, fine- and coarse-toothed combs.

Breed tip: The Cairn Terrier is not shaved short.

- Brush the coat through to remove dead hair and tangles. Often pet Cairns are never brushed by their owners, so they can respond negatively until they are used to being handled and brushed.

- With neglected coats, use a spray conditioner and lightly brush it in before grooming commences.

- Remove hair from under the feet and around the anal area with scissors.

- Where stripped (or clipped with a coarse No. 7 blade), go through the coat with the growth of the hair from the neck downwards. **1**

- Strip the untidy hairs from the back of the ears at the tip to define.

- Bathe with a mild shampoo for its natural and

therapeutic action, and use a conditioner where required.

- Dry with a blow-dryer, after toweling. The Cairn, like the Westie, really enjoys a good rub with a towel after a bath.

- Check the dog's nails, ears and teeth.

- If required, the underneath can be clipped with a No. 10 blade to remove all unnecessary hair that will trail in the mud, etc. This should be done so that it is impossible to see unless the dog rolls over on his back, and should only be done on pet dogs.

- Show Cairns should never be clipped. In fact, except for around the feet and at the end of the male dog's sheath, a blade should not go near them. Some exhibitors use thinning scissors but this usually shows as a harsh line on the coat. The Cairn, unlike the trimmed terriers, should give the impression of not having been trimmed, and this takes time and skill to achieve. Newcomers to the show ring

should seek help from an experienced exhibitor to learn how to prepare Cairns.

- Using thinning scissors, tidy the head to give an indentation between the eyes, and leaving a well-furnished round shape to the outline of the head, but in proportion to the body.

- Trim the tail upwards to balance with the stripping or clipping of the body coat.

- Check the dog's nails, ears and teeth.

DANDIE DINMONT TERRIER

COAT: The coat is a very important feature of this breed. The Dandie coat should be a mixture of two-thirds hard (not wiry) and one-third linty (not silky) hair.

The coat should be 2 inches (5 cm) long. The topknot should be soft and silky, and very pale.

MAINTENANCE: When grooming the Dandie Dinmont, only dead hair should be removed. The dogs should be hand-stripped – clipping (even in pet dogs) ruins the coat, although it is sometimes done in older dogs for ease.

LAKELAND TERRIER

For the show ring, the coat will probably be worked on twice a week to keep it in tiptop show condition and to ensure it is never out of coat. Using scissors and clippers alters the color and texture of the hair – only hand- or knife-stripping maintains the vibrant coat color and slightly wavy, harsh coat. The show dog should be hand- or knife-stripped everywhere, except for between the pads of the feet, under the stomach and where the dog may be particularly tender.

Pet owners often ask for this breed to be clipped and bring them to the salon at least every 10 to 12 weeks. Either way, this dog benefits from daily brushing.

COAT: A trimmed breed, this dog has a coat that is dense, harsh and weather-resistant, with a good undercoat.

MAINTENANCE: It requires regular brushing and grooming, as well as a complete professional strip twice a year.

PROCEDURE

Equipment needed: Slicker brush, medium-toothed comb, stripping knife, thinning scissors, scissors, clippers where applicable.

Breed tip: Should look smart at all times with the correct grooming techniques.

- Brush through the entire coat with a slicker brush, removing dead hair and tangles.

- Follow this by combing with a medium-toothed comb.

- Strip, thin or clip (with a No. 10 Oster) the head. Work from the eyebrows to the top of the skull, down the ears and from the outer corner of the eye, down the cheek to the corner of the mouth, then backwards down the throat to the neck. ▼1

- Strip, thin or clip (with a No. 7 Oster) from the skull down the neck, over the shoulder to where the legs join the body at the front. ▼1 ▼2

- Trim the chest to leave a fringe at the brisket, downwards with growth of coat to the rear, just above the hip. ▼2

- Blend the hair into the legs evenly. ▼1

- Trim the tail with the hair growth, and scissor underneath and around the anal area, or clip lightly. ▼3

- Clip under the tummy and inside the groin with a No. 10 Oster. ▼1

- Trim the hair away from between the toes and under the foot.

- Bathe the dog in a suitable shampoo and use conditioner to complement the wiry coat.

- Blow the coat dry, following the direction of the hair growth.

- Check the Lakeland's nails, ears and teeth.

- Tidy the trimmed parts where they have lifted with the bathing.

- Comb through the hair on the front legs with a slicker brush.

- Trim the foot to give a round, compact appearance.

- Lift the foot so the hair on the front leg falls naturally. Then, scissor into a cylindrical shape.

- Trim the furnishing under the chest. Work with the contours of the body, and scissor up toward the loin.

- Trim the hindlegs to blend into the body at the hip joint. ▼3

- Comb the eyebrows forward. Next, trim the hair (in the direction of the hair growth). The fall is full between and over the eyes, and from the eyebrows down, blending in with the face hair. ▼1

- Comb the beard forward to trim away any untidy hair, and to give a neat appearance.

- Note: all furnishings (e.g., face, legs, under the chest) are better trimmed by hand, not scissors. Using your thumb and forefinger, tease the hair out in the direction of growth. This maintains strong hair which is less likely to mat and tangle.

NORFOLK TERRIER

COAT: Described as shaggy, the Norfolk Terrier coat is hard and wiry. It is straight and lies close to the body, as well as being weatherproof. The hair is longer and rougher on the neck and shoulders, while the hair on the head and ears is short and smooth, except for slight whiskers and eyebrows. The ears need to be picked to keep the hair on them short.

MAINTENANCE: This dog is hand-stripped. Overtrimming is undesirable, but regular brushing on a daily basis is essential.

PROCEDURE

Equipment needed: Stripping knife, medium-toothed comb, pin brush or slicker brush.

Breed tip: Establish whether the owner likes the natural or smart look before starting.

- Brush and comb through.

- Strip the body by hand or knife, to remove any straggly hairs and to neaten its appearance to a natural-looking finish. **1**

- Bathe the dog in a mild shampoo and thoroughly rinse.

- Air-, cage- or gently blow-dry.

- Comb with a medium-toothed comb.

- Check the dog's nails, ears and teeth.

- Check between the toes for excess hair and remove with scissors.

- Both the pet and show dog will need the genital/anal area kept clean and hair-free for hygiene. The pet dog should also be scissored down the legs to neaten its appearance, as well as having the head tidied of straggly bits.

- The show dog needs constant attention to the coat, with finger-, thumb- and knife-stripping. The coat is required to be brushed frequently enough to keep it in good order, and will not be bathed as often as the pet dog.

- See also pages 205–206.

NORWICH TERRIER

Photo: Edwin.

COAT: The coat is wiry, straight and lies close to the body, with a thick undercoat. It is longer and rougher on the neck, forming a ruff to frame the face. The hair on the head is short and smooth, except for slight whiskers and eyebrows. The color is red, wheaten, black and tan, or grizzle. White marks or patches on the chest are undesirable but permissible.

MAINTENANCE: Excessive trimming to leave a sculptured look, as in some terrier breeds, is undesirable. Trimming of a different kind is required for show dogs – e.g., rolling the coat to keep a new coat growing amongst the older coat is done in most cases. Pet owners usually prefer all the old coat removed to help prevent molting hair on clothes and furniture.

PROCEDURE

Equipment needed: Pin brush/slicker brush, medium-toothed comb, stripping knife, straight-bladed scissors, thinning scissors.

Breed tip: Brush on a regular basis to keep the coat free from burrs and debris.

- Brush and comb through the coat, using a slicker or pin brush, and a medium-toothed comb.

- Strip out any loose hair with your finger and thumb or a stripping knife ▼**1**. Then work backwards from the stop to the point of the neck, and from the outside corner of the eye to where the corner of the ear joins the top of the skull. Strip straggly hairs from the ears.

- When all dead hair is removed from the body, blend into the underskirt ▼**1**. If this is more than 2 inches (5 cm) long, shorten with thinning scissors to give a smart appearance.

- Strip out hair from the front of the tail. Using thinning scissors, trim down the back of the tail and around the anus to leave a neat appearance.

- Using straight-blade scissors, cut the hair a round the outside of the feet and, underneath the feet, excessive hair growing over the pads. Remove straggly hairs from the legs.

• Bathe the dog in a good-quality, natural-ingredient shampoo.

• Air-, cage- or blow-dry the coat.

• Brush and comb through.

• Check the dog's nails, ears and teeth.

• Norfolk and Norwich Terriers are often clipped because the owners want them shortcoated. This is a shame, as they are lovely when carefully trimmed. Where the owner insists, a coarse blade is sufficient to maintain a natural look and smart appearance.

PARSON RUSSELL TERRIER

◄ *Smooth*

◄ *Broken – similar to the Smooth, but with more profuse hair around the neck and shoulders.*

▲
Rough – with the longest top coat of the three varieties.

COAT: The coat is naturally harsh, close and dense – whether Rough, Smooth or Broken – and has an undercoat. The belly and undersides are coated.

MAINTENANCE: In most cases, provided that the dog is well cared for, little maintenance is required. Once dry, dirt can be easily removed from the coat by brushing. Bathing is not recommended unless really necessary, as it can affect the coat's texture and waterproofing. This is particularly important if you show your Russell. When show Russells are stripped, it is always done by hand. They are never clipped.

Pet owners may wish their Russells to visit a grooming parlor from time to time, although it is not strictly necessary. Normally, this will be to strip the Rough variety, or to provide a bath if a pet Russell has become a little enthusiastic in the mud when out on a walk or at play. Grooming Russells normally involves little more than some stripping or clipping in order to maintain the smoothness of the coat – although coat quality in Russells is dependent on little more than good diet and overall health.

PROCEDURE

Equipment needed: Comb, bristle brush.

Breed tip: A hound glove is great at removing excess hair when the dog is shedding.

- Brush through the coat and use a fine comb to remove dead hairs.

- Strip with a serrated-edged, deep-toothed knife.

- Trim around the feet.

- Only bathe your Russell if absolutely necessary. If this is the case, make sure you use a suitable canine shampoo. At the time of molt, a hound glove can be used to remove excess hairs.

- Check the nails, ears and teeth.

SCHNAUZER (MINIATURE, STANDARD AND GIANT)

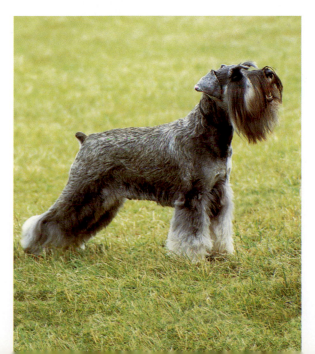

COAT: The Miniature (pictured left and ▼), Standard (▼4) and Giant (▼5) are classed as separate breeds, but their coat care and grooming requirements are the same.

The topcoat is harsh and wiry, just short enough for smartness on the body. It is slightly shorter on the neck and shoulders, but blends smoothly into the body coat. It is clean at the throat, skull, ears and under the tail. The hair on the legs is harsh. The breeds have a good undercoat.

The color is pepper and salt, black, and black and silver.

MAINTENANCE: Seen frequently in the grooming parlor. Grooming entails using many grooming skills – from hand-stripping and scissoring, clipping and blending, to rolling. The coat requires regular brushing with a slicker and combing with a medium-toothed comb, particularly on the legs and whiskers. The coat is stripped completely when it blows twice a year.

PROCEDURE

Equipment needed: Trimming scissors, two slicker brushes (one small, soft one for the face, and a harder one for the rest of the coat) and a terrier pad for the main jacket.

Breed tip: Pay attention to stripping/rolling the coat on a more regular basis to keep it looking smart all year round. Show dogs are frequently rolled every week to keep them in a full coat. Rolling consists of continually removing longer dead hairs by finger and thumb so that new coat growth is continuous. The undercoat can be kept in check by removing with a blunt stripping knife.

- Starting with the head, strip the top of the skull, the neck and the body down over the shoulder to where the front legs join the body. **1**

- Work along the back and down the back legs, to blend the coat in at a line running from the groin to the hock. **1**

- Follow the underline through to the rump and down to just above the indentation of the hock and the tail. **1**

- Trim the tail by hand- or knife-stripping (working with the direction of the hair growth). Some pet dogs are clipped. The underside of the tail is trimmed short. **2**

- Clip the ears downwards with a No. 10 Oster, or use thinning scissors to shorten the hair. Tidy the edges with scissors. **1**

- Then clip the cheeks and under the throat and down the front of the chest. **3**

- The belly can be clipped to incorporate the insides of the groin. However, leave part of the rib cage to be tapered up with scissors to make a short fringe. This will enhance the contours of the body.

- Brush the coat out using a fine spray of conditioner if dry, or where tangles are to be removed.

- Comb through the coat once more.

- Bathe in a natural-ingredient shampoo.

- Towel-dry and finish in a cage or with a blower.

- Trim with scissors under the body upwards, working with the contours of the body.

- Tidy the trimmed parts to remove stray hairs.

- Comb the eyebrows and beard forward, and scissor diagonally from the bridge of the nose to the outer corner of the eye, then scissor a small inverted V-shape between the eyes to make a distinct eyebrow and to show the stop.

- Using scissors, trim between the eyebrows into a diamond shape.

- Scissor the edges of the ears to a rectangular shape. The head should give the impression of a "house brick."

- The hair on the chest, between the legs, should now be scissored to look flat and smooth.

- Scissor the front legs to achieve a neat appearance, with the elbows close to the body, taking more hair from the outer elbow to give the appearance that the forelegs are close together, and are not sticking out.

- Scissor the feet to give them a round, catlike appearance.

- Trim the back legs, blending the longer hair into the shorter body coat.

- Pet dogs are very often clipped instead of being stripped, as this is far quicker and, therefore, cheaper. They can look extremely smart and chic when this is undertaken with consideration.

SCOTTISH TERRIER

COAT: The Scottie's coat is close-lying. It has a double coat, which consists of a short, dense undercoat and a harsh, dense and wiry outercoat that is weather-resistant.

MAINTENANCE: Requires regular brushing at least three times a week, especially the long hair of the skirt and the beard, and so on.

PROCEDURE

Equipment needed: Slicker brush, wide-toothed comb, stripping knife, clippers, scissors.

Breed tip: The Scottish Terrier presents

more work than at first appears, so give yourself more time than you initially think you'll need.

- Brush with a slicker to remove tangles and dead hair.

- Clip with a No. 10 from the eyebrows to the back of the skull to the base of the ears, down the cheek, in a line from the outer corner of the eye to the outer edge of the mouth. ▼1

- Clip a narrow strip between the eyes to within 1¹/₂ inches (4 cm) of the nose.

- Use scissors to shape the ears, leaving tufts inside at the base.

- Hand- or knife-strip, thin or clip from the head, down the neck, to leave a skirt from just above the elbow. Show dogs should not be clipped. Always remember to work in the direction of the coat growth. If stripping, remove only dead hair with a blunt stripping knife. ▼2

- Continue trimming down the back, taking in the sides of the body to a line level from just above the elbow to the bottom of the pelvis. ▼2

- Trim the upper part of tail by stripping or clipping it to tidy. ▼2

- Clip carefully under the tail and around the anal area with an Oster No. 10. When using clippers, do make sure first that the dog is not going to be shown.

- Clip the abdomen area. (Check with the owner first.)

- Clip down the front of the dog, below the throat to the breastbone, and blend in to the sides. ▼2

- Bathe the dog in a suitable shampoo, conditioning where necessary.

- Blow-dry the coat with the growth of the hair, brushing the long hair with a pin brush or slicker.

- Check the dog's nails, ears and teeth.

- Blend the skirt into the body all around. ▼2

- Trim around the feet to neaten their appearance.

- Cut the hair short between the pads and the toes.

- Comb the eyebrows and beard forward.

SEALYHAM TERRIER

COAT: The coat is long, hard and wiry with a weather-resistant undercoat.

MAINTENANCE: The dog's low carriage and long skirt attracts dirt, and grooming is required on a regular basis to keep the white or white-and-lemon coat smart.

PROCEDURE

Equipment needed: Slicker brush, wide-toothed comb, stripping knife, clippers.

Breed tip: Regular expert trimming is a must.

- Brush the coat with a slicker to remove debris and tangles.

- Comb with a wide-toothed comb.

- Strip or use thinning scissors on the head if it is not being clipped (show dogs should be stripped). Start from above the center of the eyebrow, as shown in the diagram, so the eyebrows will fall over the inner part of the eye, forwards toward the nose. Work backwards toward the back skull or the point at the top of the neck. Next, trim down from the inner corner of the eye to the edge of the mouth, and backwards to the throat. ▼1

- Trim the feet to help produce the round, catlike appearance required. Please note: the Chow is not trimmed for show purposes.

- The finished dog. 13

AKITA (JAPANESE)

COAT: The Akita is double-coated. The outer coarse coat is straight and stands off the body. The undercoat is soft and dense, and the coat on the tail is profuse.

The coat can be any color. Markings are well defined, with or without a mask or blaze.

MAINTENANCE: Regular weekly brushing will keep the coat healthy. The

ANATOLIAN SHEPHERD

COAT: It has a relatively short, dense coat with a thick undercoat. It is flat, close-lying and neither fluffy nor wavy. The coat is slightly longer and thicker at the neck, shoulder and tail, with no feathering on the ears or legs. This double coat is designed to protect the working dog against the extremes of temperature it faces on the bleak high plateau of central Turkey. The coarse outer coat naturally sheds water and mud while the dense, soft undercoat, which is slightly less thick in summer, provides insulation against the cold and sun.

All Anatolians, whether kept as working, pet or show dogs, undergo a complete molt twice a year, a process that takes two to three weeks. The outer hair is loosened and replaced gradually over this period, but the woolly undercoat is shed quite spectacularly, and can be gently plucked away in great handfuls or carefully raked out, taking care not to scratch the skin.

MAINTENANCE: This is a breed that is comparatively easy to look after. However, it looks stunning after a bath and professional groom.

PROCEDURE

Equipment needed: Bristle brush, medium-toothed comb.

Breed tip: An occasional bath will help to remove loose hair from the Anatolian's thick, dense coat.

- Brush through the entire coat with a bristle brush.

- Bathe the dog with a protein pH-balanced shampoo.

- Rinse thoroughly, taking care to ensure all soap has been removed.

- Remove any excess water from the coat while the dog is still in the bath. Follow this by drying the dog in a cage-dryer or by blow-drying. To avoid skin problems, it is important to ensure that the undercoat is not left damp after bathing.

- Check the dog's nails. The adult dog weighs about 130 pounds (60 kg) and so regular exercise on hard surfaces is normally sufficient to keep the claws naturally short. Hind dewclaws may be present and these will need regular trimming to prevent problems such as overgrowth or snagging.

- Next, check the dog's teeth and ears. Regular cleaning with antiseptic wipes will avoid irritation caused by the waxy deposit that can build up in warm, damp conditions.

CANAAN DOG

COAT: The coat is described as having a dense outercoat, harsh and straight, of short to medium length. The undercoat is close and profuse according to the season.

Color: solid-colored sand to red-brown, white or black, or spotted white with any of the aforementioned colors. Both patterns can be with or without a mask. If the dog is masked, it must be symmetrical. A black mask is permitted on all colors, and white markings are also acceptable.

MAINTENANCE: Regular brushing will keep this dog looking good.

PROCEDURE

Equipment needed: Bristle brush or slicker brush, medium-toothed comb. When the dog is molting, a grooming rake should be used, as it gets through the thick undercoat more easily than a comb or bristle brush.

Breed tip: The coat is thicker than you would imagine, so make sure it is well dried after bathing.

- Brush thoroughly with a bristle brush.

- Comb through with a medium-toothed comb to remove dead hairs.

- Bathe the dog in a natural-ingredient shampoo, and rinse well.

- Towel the excess water from the coat, then warm air- or cage-dry.

- Check the dog's nails, ears and teeth.

COLLIE (ROUGH)

COAT: The coat fits the outline of the dog's body and is very dense. The outercoat is straight and harsh to the touch. The undercoat is soft, furry and very close, almost hiding the skin. The mane and frill (neck hair) are very abundant, and the mask and face are smooth. The ears are smooth at the tips, but carry more hair toward their base. The front legs are well feathered, and the hindlegs are profusely feathered above the hocks (smooth below the hock joint). The hair on the tail is very profuse.

MAINTENANCE: Either as a pet or a show dog, regular weekly grooming will maintain the glamorous coat and featherings. It is only during a molt/shed that extra, daily grooming or a bath is required.

PROCEDURE

Equipment needed: A pure bristle brush, wide-toothed comb, scissors (thinning and blunt-nosed), water spray or spritzer, towels. A pin brush is required only during a molt.

Breed tip: Due to the nature of the double coat (the long outer hair and the thick undercoat), only a pure bristle brush should be used. The use of a pin brush on a regular basis will remove all the undercoat and spoil the elegant outline of the Collie. A coat conditioner may be added to the water spray (for pet dogs), but regular bathing is not required, as this will soften the coat and cause tangles and matted hair to collect.

- Due to the texture of the coat (which should be harsh), never groom the dog without using a fine water spray, otherwise the hair could be broken.

- Remove your dog's collar and stand your collie. Lightly spray all over with a fine water spray containing only water (for show dogs to comply with regulations), but with a coat conditioner for all other dogs.

- Towel off the coat. This will remove most surface dust and dirt. The majority of Collies will only require the feet and legs to be bathed. This can be done by standing the dog's front feet and then its back feet in a bowl of water and bathing them (see below).

- Starting at the back, while the coat is still damp, brush against the lie of the coat, lifting it in layers. Continue through, covering the front mane and frills, not forgetting the tail. By the time you have finished, a collie with the correct textured coat will be dry.

- Use a wide-toothed comb to tidy up the leg featherings and behind the ears.

- Gently comb the fine hair that grows around the ears and, if preparing for the show ring, use your thinning scissors to remove excess hair. The long, fine hair, which can grow around the back of the head, can also be removed by using finger and thumb and plucking the hair out.

- Using blunt-nosed scissors, trim around the line of the foot and remove the long hair which grows between the toes. Comb out the feathering on the hindlegs. In pet collies, this may be trimmed using scissors, cutting a line parallel to the bone. In show dogs, this is usually trimmed using thinning scissors, which gives a softer, more natural look.

- At this stage, check the length of the Collie's nails, not forgetting the dewclaws, which can be found on the front legs, just above the foot. Trim the nails with specialized nail clippers.

- During the coat molt, daily grooming will be required for all Collies. The use of a pin brush is quite acceptable at this time, as the object of this exercise is to remove all the dead undercoat to allow new hair growth. The undercoat can easily mat up at this time, especially under the elbows, around the ears, and around the hindlegs. If mats do occur, use your blunt-nosed scissors to cut into the mat, away from the skin, and loosen off the mat. A comb-through will remove most mats. A well-cared-for Collie will not mat up if regular grooming takes place.

- In the unlikely event that an allover bath is required, use a medicated or conditioning shampoo (if your Collie has rolled in something unpleasant, a medicated shampoo is preferable). Remember, though, that constant bathing will soften the coat.

- Wash the dog all over. Make sure that the water reaches the skin – the thick, woolly undercoat protects the skin and it may take some time to soak through. Protect the ears with cotton batting to stop water from entering. Shampoo and rinse thoroughly with plenty of warm water. Remove your dog from the bath and allow your Collie to shake itself dry.

- Towel down and gently brush with a bristle brush. Hand-held dryers or power blasters will hasten drying, but constant use, especially of the blaster, will speed up coat loss!

- If you are bathing to remove dead coat, using a pin brush will quicken coat loss, especially if used two to three days after a bath.

- The addition of any coloring (blue whiteners, etc.) is not permitted for shows, but may be used at home to enhance the white.

- Finally, don't forget to remove the cotton batting from the ears and to check the condition of the ears, eyes and teeth.

ESTRELA MOUNTAIN DOG

COAT: There are two types – long and short. The outercoat on the long variety is thick and moderately harsh, resembling goat hair. It lies close over the body, and is flat or slightly wavy, never curly. The undercoat is very dense and normally lighter in color. The hair is short and smooth on the head, and abundant around the neck and chest, forming a ruff. The short coat variety is thick, moderately harsh and straight, with a shorter undercoat.

MAINTENANCE: Needs regular brushing.

PROCEDURE

Equipment needed: Pin, slicker or bristle brush, a medium-toothed comb and a good rake.

Breed tip: Do not overlook the grooming needs of the short-coated variety, which requires as much regular attention as the long coats.

- Brush with a pin, slicker or bristle brush.

- Comb through to remove dead hairs.

- If bathing is undertaken, use a natural-based shampoo and be careful to rinse thoroughly.

- Dry with absorbent towels.

- A good rake should be used to remove the shedding coat when the dog molts.

- Check the dog's nails, ears and teeth.

- Check for clogged hair under the pads and remove with scissors.

FINNISH LAPPHUND

COAT: The coat is profuse. The outercoat is long and coarse, the undercoat soft and thick. The coat is shorter on the head and the front parts of the legs.

The coat comes in all colors, but the main color must dominate.

MAINTENANCE: The Finnish Lapphund needs regular brushing, especially when kept mostly in the house as a family pet. However, an outdoor type of family will suit it better.

PROCEDURE

Equipment needed: Slicker brush, wide-toothed comb.

Breed tip: Some Finnish Lapphunds seem to have a deep-seated fear of water, perhaps relating to the fact that a wet dog could quickly become a dead dog in the freezing Finnish conditions its ancestors endured.

To prevent this from becoming a problem, be organized when grooming this breed. Before you begin, make sure you have everything on hand that you will need, to minimize the length of time during which your Lapphund is wet. If you don't, the dog will roll and shake itself excessively following bathing.

• Comb through the entire coat with a wide-toothed comb, removing any excessive and molting coat.

• Brush the entire coat with a slicker, brushing upwards and then downwards to remove dead hair.

• Bathe the dog in a good-quality, natural-ingredient shampoo, such as tea tree and lavender.

• No conditioner should be used on the Finnish Lapphund's coat – just rinse the coat well, taking care to remove all the soap. The coat should be clean, healthy and have a matte finish.

• After rinsing, towel the coat well and finish with a normal blower. Make sure the dryer blows the hair and not the skin, or it will be very uncomfortable for your Finnish Lapphund.

• Remember to check the dog's nails, ears and teeth.

• Check underneath the feet for clogged hair, and remove only the minimum of hair with scissors. Otherwise, the dog should be left natural – never trimmed elsewhere on the body.

FINNISH SPITZ

COAT: The coat on the head and on the front of its straight legs is short and close. On the body and the back of the legs it is longish, semi-erect, and is stiffer on the neck and back. The outercoat on the shoulders is considerably longer and coarser. The hair is longer and denser on the back of the thighs and on the tail. The undercoat is short, soft and dense. The color is reddish brown or red gold, preferably bright.

MAINTENANCE: No trimming is necessary, but brushing is a must.

PROCEDURE

Equipment needed: Slicker brush, wide- or medium-toothed comb.

Breed tip: As with all Spitz breeds, brush against the lie of the coat.

- Brush the coat, and then comb through with a wide-toothed comb.

- Bathe only when necessary. Use a natural shampoo and rinse well.

- Check the dog's nails, ears and teeth.

- Run over the coat with velvet or a silk pad.

GERMAN SHEPHERD DOG

COAT: The German Shepherd Dog has a thick, double coat. Some have long coats.

MAINTENANCE: The German Shepherd's coat is relatively easy to maintain and looks positively sparkling after a bath. Regular brushing will keep it in great condition.

PROCEDURE

Equipment needed: Curry or slicker brush, medium-toothed comb.

Breed tip: The dog can lose so much hair that it is best to groom it outside (in fair weather) or in a noncarpeted room.

• Brush the body hair thoroughly with a curry brush or slicker to remove dead hair.

• Bathe the dog in a pH-alkaline balanced shampoo or with a purifying shampoo and mask.

• Blow the coat with a blaster to remove excess water.

• Finish the drying process with a blower, or air- or cage-dry.

• Check the dog's nails, ears and teeth.

• Brush the coat with a sisal brush and, if necessary, lightly spray with coat conditioner.

GERMAN SPITZ

COAT: Its coat is double and consists of a soft, woolly undercoat and a long harsh-textured, perfectly straight topcoat covering the whole of the body.

The hair is very abundant around the neck and forequarters with a frill of profuse off-standing straight hair extending over the shoulders.

In some countries, there are color restrictions – contact your national kennel club or breed association for details of the breed standard.

MAINTENANCE: Grooming should be regular and thorough, but the coat is easy to maintain.

PROCEDURE

Equipment needed: Slicker brush, medium- or wide-toothed comb.

Breed tip: The German Spitz is not a trimmed breed, although some breeders do tend to tidy the hair on the hock and around the feet.

• Brush through the entire coat with a slicker brush or pin brush, removing mats and dead coat.

• Bathe the dog in a suitable good-quality shampoo.

• Rinse thoroughly, ensuring that all soap has been removed.

• Apply a conditioner and again rinse thoroughly.

• Blow the coat dry, brushing with a pin brush.

• Don't forget to check the dog's nails, ears and teeth.

228

GREAT PYRENEES (PYRENEAN MOUNTAIN DOG)

COAT: The coat consists of a profuse undercoat of very fine hair and an outercoat of longer, coarser-textured hair that is weather-resistant. The coat is thick, straight or slightly wavy, but it is never curly or fuzzy.

The Great Pyrenees color is mainly white with patches of badger, wolf gray or pale yellow.

MAINTENANCE: This breed needs thorough grooming at least once a week. In addition, the Great Pyrenees should always be groomed thoroughly before bathing.

PROCEDURE

Equipment needed: Pin brush, wide-toothed comb and a fine-toothed comb (the finer-toothed version is for knots around the ears).

Breed tip: A huge breed, the Great Pyrenees

puppy must get used to grooming from a young age; persuading a reluctant adult to be bathed is not an easy feat.

- Brush through the entire coat with a pin brush. Be extra vigilant at getting underneath the body and in the breeches, as you must ensure you remove dead hairs that will otherwise cause clogging.

- After brushing, comb with a wide-toothed comb.

- Bathe the dog in a white-enhancing shampoo (but use an ordinary shampoo before a show, as most kennel club rules state that no substance is allowed to be used that will alter the coat).

- Rinse thoroughly.

- If possible, allow the dog to shake a good deal of the water from its coat.

- Towel-dry with a superabsorbent towel.

- After removing the excess moisture with a towel, use a domestic hair-dryer to dry the rest of the coat. While you are drying the coat, smooth down the hair with the brush so the topcoat lies close and flat to the undercoat.

- Complete the drying process with warm air or with a blower.

- Do not forget to check the dog's nails, ears and teeth.

- Finally, brush over the coat once again, using a spray conditioner if required.

GREENLAND DOG

COAT: Thick, double coat, consisting of an impenetrable undercoat and protruding outercoat of coarser hair.

MAINTENANCE: Brushing is all that is required for this breed, together with an occasional bath.

PROCEDURE

Equipment needed: Bristle brush, wire brush, medium-toothed and wide-toothed combs.

Breed tip: Never underestimate the Greenland Dog's size and weight – you may need to enlist help for bathtimes.

• Brush through with a bristle brush.

• Next, comb to remove dead hairs.

• Bathe when required in a natural-ingredient shampoo, and rinse well.

• Towel-dry and then finish in warm air or a cage.

• Check the dog's nails, ears and teeth.

• For show dogs, towel off, use a blaster to remove all excess water and any remaining loose coat, then blow-dry to finish.

HOVAWART

COAT: The coat is long in appearance, but is short on the face and front legs, and is not as long on the rib cage and the thighs. It has a fine, light undercoat, which is straight or slightly waved. The color is black/gold, black or blond.

MAINTENANCE: Relatively easy to look after, only requiring regular brushing and the occasional bath. Trimming is done only on the feet.

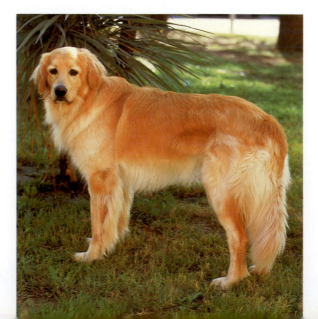

PROCEDURE

Equipment needed: Curry brush or slicker brush, wide-toothed comb.

Breed tip: For the show ring, bathe the Hovawart well in advance, leaving enough time for the coat to settle.

• Brush through the entire coat with a curry brush or slicker.

• Comb with a wide-toothed comb.

• Bathe the dog in a natural-ingredient shampoo.

• Rinse thoroughly, ensuring that all the shampoo has been removed.

• The coat can be blow-dried after using a light conditioner to enhance the coat and to prevent dryness.

• Check the dog's nails, ears and teeth.

• Check underneath the feet for excess hair and remove with scissors.

• The feet can be trimmed round with scissors to enhance their oval, well-arched appearance.

JAPANESE SPITZ

COAT: It has a profuse standoff outercoat and a thick, short, dense undercoat, which is soft in texture. The mane on the neck and shoulders reaches down to the brisket. The tail is profusely covered with long hair and is curled over the back. The hair on the face is shorter, as it is on the ears, on the front of the forelegs, the hindlegs and below the hock.

MAINTENANCE: Regular brushing is essential.

PROCEDURE

Equipment needed: Pin brush or slicker, wide-toothed comb.

Breed tip: Should the dog get muddy and dirty, do not try to brush or wash him clean. Wait for the mud to dry, brush, and the mud will fall off the hair, leaving it white and clean.

• Brush the coat thoroughly with a pin brush or slicker. Brushing against the lie of the coat keeps it clean and dust-free.

• Comb with a wide-toothed comb.

• Bathe in a white-enhancing shampoo and apply a suitable white conditioner for that extra sparkle. (Prior to a show, no coat-enhancing substances should be used, of course.)

• Blow-dry while brushing the coat with a pin brush.

- Remember to check the dog's nails, ears and teeth.

- Use thinners to tidy any straggly hair from the hocks.

- Trim hairs under and around the feet to give them a catlike appearance.

- Check under the feet for excess hair and trim with scissors to prevent clogging.

KEESHOND

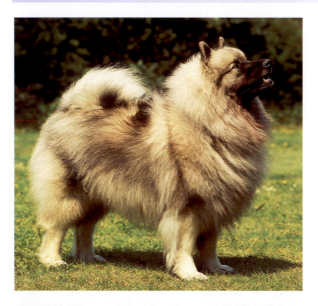

COAT: The coat is a harsh, standoff and straight one. It has a dense ruff and is well feathered on the forelegs. The trousers are profuse. The Keeshond is not feathered below the hocks. It has a soft, thick, light-colored undercoat.

MAINTENANCE: Less arduous than it appears. Brush regularly with a pin brush or slicker and comb out dead hairs.

PROCEDURE

Equipment needed: Bristle or nylon brush (with the bristles well spaced – not close), and a wide, long-toothed comb.

Breed tip: Easier to keep groomed than its coat would have you believe.

- Brush the coat in layers, right down to the skin. Do this by first brushing toward the tail and then finish by brushing toward the head.

- Comb the feathering and hocks.

- Trim around the feet to give them a catlike appearance, and check under the feet and remove excess hair between the pads.

- Check the dog's nails, ears and teeth.

- Tidy the hocks with scissors.

- Use a comb only when the dog is molting, to remove loose undercoat.

- Bathing is seldom necessary as the coat is not oily. If the coat gets muddy, let it dry and then it can be brushed out easily. Bathing softens the coat, which is not desirable in the show ring and makes it less easy to keep.

- If a bath is unavoidable (e.g., if the dog has a skin infection), use a shampoo recommended by your vet, and rinse thoroughly.

- Blow-dry, brushing the hair away from the heat and not blowing the skin.

- For showing, the feet, stomach and sometimes the trousers are bathed with a harsh-coat shampoo. A pin brush can be used on the ruff, trousers and tail plume at the very last minute before going into the show ring (used more, it will remove too much undercoat).

KUVASZ (HUNGARIAN)

COAT: The Kuvasz coat is pure white. It has a slight wave and is double-coated, with a medium-coarse topcoat and a fine, woolly undercoat.

MAINTENANCE: Regular brushing is required, and perhaps a bath.

PROCEDURE

Equipment needed: Slicker brush, wide-toothed comb.

Breed tip: Be prepared for profuse shedding in warm weather.

• Brush the entire coat with a slicker to remove dead hairs.

• Follow by combing with a wide-toothed comb.

• Bathe the dog in a tea tree and lavender or protein-balanced shampoo.

• Rinse well, leaving no trace of shampoo suds in the thick coat.

• Towel-dry, then blow-dry with warm air or use a cage-dryer or a blower.

• Don't forget to check the dog's nails, ears and teeth.

LEONBERGER

COAT: The coat is medium-soft to hard, fairly long and lies close to the body, despite a good undercoat.
  Slightly wavy, but never curled, the coat is very evident on the mane, throat and chest, and the color is light yellow, golden to red-brown.

MAINTENANCE: The Leonberger's coat requires regular brushing to keep it in good condition.

PROCEDURE

Equipment needed: Slicker brush, metal comb.

Breed tip: It is very important to get the Leonberger puppy used to regular grooming, before it grows!

• Brush through the coat with a slicker brush.

• Comb with a metal comb.

• Bathe only as necessary. Use a good-quality proprietary shampoo. Rinse thoroughly.

• Remove excess water with absorbent towels or blast out with a power blower.

• Finish the drying process by using warm air or a blower.

• Brush through the coat with a slicker.

• Check the dog's nails, ears and teeth.

MAREMMA SHEEPDOG

COAT: The dog's coat fits its outline and is long, plentiful and rather harsh. It has a slight waviness but curliness is not permitted. The coat forms a thick ruff on the neck. A thick, close undercoat is present, especially in winter.

   The color is usually all white.

MAINTENANCE: Requires regular brushing. The coat sheds once or twice a year.

PROCEDURE

Equipment needed: Bristle brush/slicker, medium-toothed comb.

Breed tip: A white-enhancing shampoo is a useful addition to the grooming collection (though, given show regulations, it should not be used on show dogs).

• Brush the entire coat with a bristle brush.

• Use a comb to remove excess undercoat.

• Bathe the Maremma in a white-enhancing shampoo (only for pet dogs – show dogs should not have their coat altered) and rinse well to ensure all suds are removed.

• Remove excess water from the coat with a superabsorbent towel, or use a power blower.

• Finish the dog in warm air or a cage, or with a blower.

• Check the dog's ears and nails, and clean and trim where necessary.

• Finally, brush its teeth.

NEWFOUNDLAND

COAT: Double, flat, dense, coarse and oily.

MAINTENANCE: This water-resistant coat is extremely time-consuming.

PROCEDURE

Equipment needed: Slicker brush, wide-toothed comb.

Breed tip: Early socialization and an introduction to grooming is essential.

- Brush through the coat from root to tip with a slicker brush to remove dead hairs.

- Comb with a wide-toothed comb.

- Bathe in a protein pH-balanced shampoo, and rinse thoroughly.

- Blow excess water from the coat with a power blower or let the dog shake outside if the air is warm enough. Then power-dry.

- Newfies have hair that grows under and over the ear, which should be trimmed (to let air circulate and to prevent infection, and so that the ear looks neat and tidy). The excess hair around the ear flap should be trimmed, following the natural curve of the ear. Then the long hair over the flap can be slightly trimmed, using thinning scissors – only take a little hair off at a time, so there is less chance of making a terrible mistake. This will create more of a natural appearance. Thinning scissors can be used on other parts if needed.

- Check the dog's nails, ears and teeth.

- Check between the pads for matted, excess hair and remove.

- Trim the anal area, if necessary.

- Spray with a coat-protecting conditioner – obviously, show dogs cannot have anything applied to the coat.

- Extra grooming is required during molting.

NORWEGIAN BUHUND

COAT: The Buhund's coat is harsh but smooth, and the undercoat is soft and woolly.

MAINTENANCE: A breed that is easy to keep clean.

PROCEDURE

Equipment needed: Bristle brush, medium-toothed comb.

Breed tip: In common with other Spitz breeds, the Norwegian Buhund enjoys a good chat with other dogs – something to bear in mind if you run a salon. If you have a Buhund booked in, avoid having other known "barkers" scheduled for that morning or afternoon, or you could end up with a headache!

• Brush through the entire coat with a bristle brush.

• Comb to remove dead hairs.

• Bathe the dog in a natural shampoo, and rinse well.

• Towel-dry and finish with warm air or a blower, or cage-dry.

• Remember to check the dog's nails, ears and teeth.

NORWEGIAN ELKHOUND

COAT: This most attractive hound has a close, abundant and weather-resistant coat, with a soft, woolly undercoat that will molt profusely. The coat is short and smooth on the head and front legs, and longest on the neck, back of the thighs and the tail.

The color is gray or various shades with black tips to the outer coat. It is lighter on the chest, stomach, legs, underside of the tail, buttocks and in a harness mark (a darker patch across the body). The ears and foreface are dark, with a dark line from the eye to the ear being desirable. The undercoat is pure pale gray.

MAINTENANCE: The coat is not trimmed, but will benefit from a bath at molting time to help rid it of all the dead hairs.

A bitch sheds twice a year, just prior to a season; males will shed around once a year. They do not necessarily shed in the summer, as the thick undercoat insulates against heat as well as cold. Requires regular brushing.

PROCEDURE

Equipment needed: Slicker brush, wide-toothed comb.

Breed tip: Keep the Elkhound groomed regularly unless you want a heap of hair on the carpet!

• Thoroughly brush the coat with a slicker and remove dead hairs with a medium-toothed comb.

- Bathe as necessary, using a good-quality shampoo.

- Rinse thoroughly, making sure all the soap has been removed.

- These dogs usually shake off the excess water, and the coat can then be dried with a towel.

- In the United States, the dogs are often bathed prior to a show, and the coat is dried by blasting out the excess water (where the dog will tolerate the high-velocity blower). Otherwise, use superabsorbent paper towels.

American owners also generally blow-dry the coat, while brushing with a pin brush or slicker. However, this is not done in Europe and the U.K.

- Brush and comb through the coat with a light spray of stay-in-the-coat conditioner.

- Do not forget that show dogs are not permitted to have any coat-altering substances used on their coats.

- Do not forget to check the Elkhound's nails, ears and teeth. Clean the ears and teeth as necessary, and trim the nails if they have grown too long.

NORWEGIAN LUNDEHUND

COAT: It has a dense, rough outercoat with a soft undercoat. The coat is short on the head and front legs, and is longer on the neck and thighs.

The color is reddish brown to fallow, preferably with black tips on the hairs. Black or gray are also acceptable. All colors with white markings or white with dark markings.

MAINTENANCE: Fairly easy to maintain with regular brushing.

PROCEDURE

Equipment needed: Bristle brush, medium-toothed comb.

Breed tip: A quick once-over with a sisal brush or cloth after grooming will give the coat a marvelous gleam.

- Brush the coat thoroughly with a bristle brush.

- Comb out the dead hair.

- Bathe the dog, if required, with a natural-ingredient shampoo, and rinse well.

- Use an absorbent towel to take away excess moisture from the coat and finish the drying process with warm air.

- Check the dog's nails, ears and teeth.

POMERANIAN

COAT: The coat is made up of an undercoat and an outercoat. The former is soft and fluffy; the latter is long, straight and harsh, and covers the whole of the body.

The coat is very abundant around the neck and the fore part of the shoulders and chest, forming a frill that extends over the shoulder. The forequarters are well feathered, and the thighs and hindlegs are well feathered to the hocks.

MAINTENANCE: It needs regular attention to keep it clean and attractive. Thorough brushing, checking nails, cleaning ears and teeth, and trimming should be done once a week.

Males cast their coats once a year and bitches twice a year (usually after a season), ending up looking quite sorry for themselves. Do not worry, it will grow back, sometimes better than ever.

PROCEDURE

Equipment needed: Slicker/pin brush, medium-toothed metal comb, scissors, cotton buds.

Breed tip: Brush against the lie of the coat to give the Pomeranian its round pompom appearance.

• Brush the coat with the slicker/pin brush. Work from the top of the head, layering the hair as you go and making sure you reach skin level.

• Next, work through the coat with the comb. If you encounter any tangles, try to tease them out gently using finger and thumb or a comb. If you need to use scissors, cut down

the length of the knot – not across – to ensure minimal coat loss.

• A bath should only be considered when the dog is out of coat – when in coat, use a dry shampoo. For a wet bath, use a suitable pH-alkaline-balanced shampoo, rinsing carefully.

• Blow-dry the hair. Work from the head, layering the hair as you go. Brush as you dry.

• Check the dog's nails and clean its ears and teeth.

• Trim the hair with thinning shears or scissors from the hocks in order to give a smooth finish.

• Trim the hair from under the feet where necessary, tidying around the feet to give them a catlike appearance.

• The hair around the anus should also be trimmed for hygiene reasons.

SAMOYED

COAT: The body coat is thick and close, with a soft and short undercoat. It has harsh (but not wiry) hairs growing through it, forming a water-resistant outercoat, that stands away straight and is free from curl.

MAINTENANCE: This thick, luxuriant coat requires much attention, but the dog looks magnificent when well turned out.

Samoyeds shed their coats periodically and will require extra grooming during this time.

PROCEDURE

Equipment needed: Pin brush, wide-toothed comb.

Breed tip: This dog is worth all the attention that its coat requires.

- Brush through the coat with a pin brush to remove dead hairs.

- Comb with a medium- or wide-toothed comb.

- Bathe in a superwhite enhancing shampoo to help remove stains or discoloring, applying a nourishing white conditioner. Remember that for the show ring no substances must be used on the coat.

- Blast excess water from the coat and blow-dry.

- Check the Samoyed's nails, ears and teeth.

SCHIPPERKE

COAT: It has a typically crisp, dense coat, which is abundant. It is smooth on the head, ears and legs, and lies close on the back and side.

The Schipperke's coat is erect and thick around the neck, forming a mane, ruff and frill, and there are good culottes on the back of the thighs.

MAINTENANCE: The Schipperke is easy to maintain.

PROCEDURE

Equipment needed: Pin brush or slicker, wide- or medium-toothed comb.

Breed tip: The tight-fitting coat makes this an easy dog to keep clean.

- Brush with a pin brush or slicker, removing dead hairs.

- Bathe in a suitable pH-balanced shampoo.

- Rinse thoroughly.

- Apply a quality conditioner to add that extra sparkle to the Schipperke's dark coat.

- Blow the coat dry, following the hair growth.

- Check the dog's nails, ears and teeth.

SHIBA INU (JAPANESE)

COAT: The coat is thick. It has a hard, straight outercoat, with a soft, dense undercoat. The hair on the tail is slightly longer.

The Shiba Inu color is red, black, black and tan, or brindle. White with red or gray tinge.

MAINTENANCE: Easy to maintain, with only regular brushing required to keep the dog looking smart and clean.

PROCEDURE

Equipment needed: Slicker brush, wide-toothed comb.

Breed tip: Don't neglect to gently brush the tail, which has slightly longer hair than on the rest of the body.

- Brush through the entire coat with a slicker brush. Brush in the opposite way to how you would normally groom – i.e., brush toward the head. Along the top of the back, however, brush toward the tail.

- Next, comb the coat with a wide-toothed comb to remove dead hairs.

- Bathe the dog in a natural shampoo, and rinse thoroughly.

- If necessary, condition the coat with a light cream to suit the coat texture, and rinse out thoroughly.

- Remove excess water from the coat with an absorbent towel and finish by drying with warm air, in a cage or with a light blower.

- Check the nails, ears and teeth.

SIBERIAN HUSKY

COAT: The Siberian has a double coat, which is medium in length, giving the dog a well-furred appearance. The undercoat is soft and dense. Guard hairs of the outercoat are straight and smooth-lying, never harsh, rough or shaggy.

MAINTENANCE: It is easy to groom with regular weekly brushing with a bristle brush. Comb out dead and molting hairs with a medium-toothed comb.

If you have any difficulty with the coat or require more specialist supervision, contact your breed club for advice.

PROCEDURE

Equipment needed: Bristle brush, medium-toothed comb.

Breed tip: A heavy molter, the Siberian will need regular grooming to collect loose hair and to minimize that which accumulates on your carpet or furniture.

- Brush with a slicker brush if the dog is molting, or use a bristle brush. Then comb through with a medium-toothed comb. The undercoat will fall out during molting.

- Bathe the dog in a suitable, quality pH-balanced shampoo and apply a conditioner.

- Blow-dry the coat.

- Check the dog's nails, ears and teeth.

- Trim the feet to look oval and compact, if required.

ST. BERNARD

The St. Bernard coat comes in shorthaired (left) and longhaired (right) varieties.

COAT: There are two coat types. Longhaired dogs have a dense, flat coat that is rather fuller around the neck and the thighs, and the tail is well feathered. Shorthaired have a close, houndlike coat, with slight feathering on the thighs and tail.

MAINTENANCE: This is a dog with a fair acreage of coat to be groomed.

PROCEDURE

Equipment needed: Slicker brush, medium- or wide-toothed comb.

Breed tip: The St. Bernard generally loves being bathed and brushed, but don't take any chances – get it used to being groomed from a young age. Because of its size, a helper may be required.

- Brush the dog with a slicker to remove dead hairs.

- Comb with a medium- or wide-toothed comb.

- Bathe the dog in a suitable shampoo, using white-enhancing shampoo on white parts to give a finish of splendor. Do not use any shampoo that will affect the coat if you intend to show your dog.

- A purifying shampoo and mask can be used three times a year, if required, for that extra-special finish – but is not for frequent use.

- Blast the excess water from the coat with a power dryer or use superabsorbent towels.

- Then blow-dry.

- Don't forget to check the St. Bernard's nails, ears and teeth.

- Remove untidy hairs on the hocks with thinning shears.

- Additional trimming of the hair on the feet is sometimes required on the longhaired variety.

- The ears need plucking and the underline should be tidied with scissors.

- With the show dog, consideration must be given to the condition of the coat when bathing, as too much undercoat may be pulled out, leaving the dog looking short of coat.

SWEDISH LAPPHUND

COAT: The coat is weather-resistant, with the hair standing straight out from the body. It is short on the head and front legs, and longer on the brisket, thigh and tail. There is a ruff around the neck. The undercoat is dense and finely curled.

The color is bear-brown, black, brown and a combination of black and brown. A white mark on the chest, white feet and a white tip on the tail are acceptable.

MAINTENANCE: Relatively easy to maintain with regular brushing.

PROCEDURE

Equipment needed: Slicker brush and a wide-toothed comb.

Breed tip: A bristle brush can be used on the softer puppy coat.

- Brush the entire dog with a slicker.

- Comb with a wide-toothed comb.

- Bathe the dog in a natural shampoo, and rinse well.

- Dry with a blower, brushing the hair away from the direction of the heat with a pin brush.

- Check the dog's nails, ears and teeth.

- Check under the pads for excess hair and remove with scissors, if necessary.

- Brush the coat once more, adding a fine sheen spray to enhance the coat.

TIBETAN MASTIFF

COAT: The males carry more coat than the females. It is fairly long, thick and woolly, with a heavy undercoat in cold weather. The hair is fine but straight, and never silky, curly or wavy. There is a heavy undercoat, giving a manelike appearance. The tail is bushy and densely coated.
   Color: rich black, gold, black and tan, brown, various shades of gray, and blue tan.

MAINTENANCE: Low maintenance – just needs a weekly brush. The breed molts only once a year on average (in the spring).

PROCEDURE

Equipment needed: Slicker brush, wide-toothed comb.

Breed tip: It is essential to get the puppy used to grooming to prevent problems later.

- Brush through the entire coat with a slicker brush.

- Comb with a wide-toothed comb.

- If it is necessary to bathe the dog, use a natural-ingredient shampoo.

- Rinse thoroughly, making sure that all suds have been removed.

- Blast water from the coat or use super-absorbent towels, and leave the dog to dry naturally.

- Check the dog's nails, ears and teeth.

- Clip down the cheeks to produce a clean appearance, tightening the skin where necessary to ensure a smooth finish and so as not to catch loose skin. ▼3 ▼5

- Clip under the chin ▼6, down the neck to the chest in a V-shape to each side of the chest bone. ▼3

- The coat on the body is clipped, stripped, carded or thinned according to requirement (i.e., if it is a pet or show dog), but the shape is the same ▼7. Make a visual line between the chest bone and the bottom of the pelvis, and work from the neck down to this line. Leave a profuse skirt, which will almost reach to the ground in dogs whose coats are significantly groomed. ▼8

- Trim the tail upwards, away from the body. ▼8 ▼9

- Clean off the hair from around the anus by clipping with an Oster No. 10, or by shortening the hair with scissors.

▼1

▼2

▶3

▼4

▼5

▼6

- Bathe the dog in a protein shampoo. ▽10

- Rinse thoroughly and apply conditioner.

- Blow the hair dry, brushing with a pin brush or slicker. ▽11

- Lightly spray with a coat-enhancer and brush through. ▽12

- Check the dog's nails, ears and teeth.

- Trim the feet to a round shape and clip out the hair from under the pads. ▽13

- Trim the bottom of the leg to give a bell-bottom appearance. ▽8

- Blend in the clipped neck area to the shoulder, making the shoulder clean by shortening the hair to accentuate the outline. ▽8

- Blend in the body skirt to a harmonious look without any appearance of a doorstep effect between the body and the skirt. Pay particular attention to the clipped area at the rear to ensure this is well blended. ▽8

- Bring the hair on the ear fringe down. Hold it in your fingers and trim lightly across with curved scissors to enhance the look, rather than to shorten the hair to any degree.

- Strip the topknot where possible, depending on the coat texture and depending on whether the dog will be shown. Blend in with thinning scissors. Brush the hair first to one side. Then trim, using thinning scissors or by clipping with an Oster No. 10 with the growth of the hair. Then brush the hair to the other side and trim back. Then brush over the top to give a clean appearance.

- The hair at the edge of the skirt is leveled to appear neat. Remember, this dog should appear stunning.

- The finished dog. ▽14

7

8

BEDLINGTON TERRIER

COAT: The coat is described as thick and "linty" and needs regular trimming, as it does not molt like most other breeds and is therefore a good breed for those allergic to dog hair, such as asthmatics. Standing well out from the skin, the hair is crisp and has a distinct tendency to twist, particularly on the head and face.

MAINTENANCE: The Bedlington should be trimmed on a regular four- to six-week basis to keep it smart and to prevent the dead hair from becoming tangled and matted. In addition, the dog should be thoroughly combed every two to three days, or its coat will quickly become matted.

PROCEDURE

Equipment needed: Slicker brush, wide- or medium-toothed comb, clippers, scissors.

Breed tip: Professional trimming is advisable unless the owner takes the trouble to learn the lengthy art of grooming. As a general rule, the coat trim and overall shape of the Bedlington should be a series of curves, with no harsh transitions between different lengths of coat.

- Brush through with a slicker brush and a comb.

- If the hair is dirty, it can be blown through with a power blower to remove grime and dirt, and to reduce matting. Note: A freshly washed coat will stand away from the skin, making the hair easier to trim.

- Depending on the predetermined length of hair to remain, use an Oster No. 10 or No. 15 against the grain of growth to clip the side of the face. Follow a line starting from the back corner of the eye to the front edge of the ear, and another from the back corner of the eye to the outer edge of the mouth. **1**

- Clip the ears to leave a diamond-shaped tassel of hair. **1**

- Clip the chin and underjaw down to the base of the throat, forming a V-shape to a point half way between the Adam's apple and the breastbone. Use a No. 10 or No. 15 Oster, as on the cheeks. **2**

- Depending on the style of trim preferred, you will need to clip the hair on the back of the head slightly differently. For the traditional "U.K. trim," use a No. 5 Oster to trim the hair off the neck, starting from the back of the skull and moving down to the withers. For a more "U.S.-style" trim, also use a No. 5 Oster, but clip with the grain of the hair, starting from the base of the ear and progressing diagonally toward the center of the base of the neck, forming a V-shape of hair down the neck.

impossible to remove without cutting. On occasions, it has been necessary to put a filthy, dirty Bichon into the bath and put in spray conditioner (anti-tangle or dematter) while the dog is soaking wet, and brush out the mats with the mat-breaker. This is avoidable if the dog is well combed before bathing.

• Try to split the felts by parting small sections at a time with your fingertips, and by spraying in an untangle product or a dematter.

• Brush with a slicker and comb through with a wide-toothed comb.

• Bathe regularly, at least once a month, in an appropriate shampoo, being careful to use a good-quality conditioner. Sometimes, add a teaspoonful of baby oil or similar to the conditioner, to help prevent the coat from drying out.

• Rinse thoroughly. The Bichon may need two shampoos to get it clean.

• Not all groomers consider it necessary, but many choose to brush through the dog's wet coat hair with a slicker brush before beginning blow-drying.

• Blow-dry the hair after using absorbent towels to lightly swab up excess moisture. Professional groomers and showdog owners will use a high-velocity hair-dryer to first remove excess moisture (it does not dry the coat). Then, a dryer with variable heat/ strength settings will be used to dry the coat while brushing.

• Starting with the tail, dry only small sections at a time, brushing continuously with a slicker or bristle brush. Next, brush and dry the legs, followed by the body hair and then the head and ears. Make sure you comb the hair away from the body. If you are aiming for the show-quality "powderpuff" effect, it

is important to ensure that all the hair has been thoroughly groomed while drying, so the Bichon's natural curl is brushed out into a soft-textured, straighter puff.

• Comb through the coat before trimming, taking care to brush the hair up, away from the coat. The coat should be combed constantly while trimming.

• If you are scissoring for the first time without the aid of an experienced groomer, look carefully at the photograph on page 251. Try to copy the perfect rounded appearance.

• The ears are so well blended, it is hard to distinguish them. It may be necessary to use thinning scissors underneath the ears if aiming for a show-standard finish.

• Trim excess hair from under the feet.

• Trim the hair from under and around the anus, leaving the tail hair long.

• Scissor the rear legs, always keeping the scissors parallel to the body. When viewed from behind, the dog's legs should resemble a straight-sided, upside-down letter U. 1

• Next, trim the body hair. Begin with the sides and move down and underneath the body.

• Scissor the front legs to look straight when viewed from the front, but cylindrical (roller-shaped) from a distance. The feet are included in this line, hidden by the continuous line of leg hair. 2

• The hair on the topline – along the back from the shoulder to the tail – should be level, and closer than the hair on the neck. Scissor, following the line of the body, to give a round appearance, taking care to blend in well with the neck hair. 3

• If necessary, retrim the hindquarters and body hair to give a well-blended appearance. 1

• Excess hair should be removed from the inside of the dog's ear leathers, using your fingers or blunt tweezers and removing only a little at a time. Blend in the remaining hair with the Bichon's characteristic topknot. 2

• The hair over the eyes is combed forward and trimmed back to allow full view of the eyes. Keeping the scissor ends away from the dog's eyes, start by removing the hair on the inside corners of the eyes. 2

• Neaten over the bridge of the nose, combing the remainder downward. 2

• Comb the topknot and trim to a smooth, rounded appearance, also trimming any hair falling over the top of the eyes.

• The line across the chin, incorporating the beard, is fairly straight. The beard hair should be blended with the ear furnishings, and the neck blended with the topline (see below). 2

• Give a final comb through and check the dog's nails, ears and teeth.

BLACK RUSSIAN TERRIER

COAT: The whole body is covered with a thick, tough coat, with decorative hair well defined on the head and limbs. The mustache and beard are features, and give the muzzle a blunt, rectangular shape. The hair is rough and thick, with a fold (crinkle), which, when pulled straight, will make the hair appear longer. The body hair is shortened to about 2 to 4 inches (4 to 10 cm). The front and rear legs are well protected by slightly longer rough hair. The color is black, or black with an insignificant amount of gray hair.

MAINTENANCE: Trimming is obligatory in accordance with the approved style. Regular brushing is essential (at least three times a week). Bathing and caring for the coat, keeping it in the desired attractive style, is usually done by an expert.

PROCEDURE

Equipment needed: Slicker brush, wide-toothed comb, scissors or clippers.

Breed tip: As this dog molts slightly, it is essential that it receives regular grooming.

• Brush through the entire coat with a slicker brush, lifting the coat to brush the hair in sections to ensure this is done thoroughly.

• Comb with a wide-toothed comb.

• Bathe in a suitable, natural shampoo that will not remove too much of the natural oil from the coat.

• Dry the dog with superabsorbent towels. Brush or comb through, and then finish with a blower or in a cage.

• Starting with the head: trim the ears from the fold of the ears to the tip by clipping downwards (away from the head) with an Oster No. 10 blade (or equivalent) or scissors. Trim on the inside and outside. Tidy the edge with scissors, while holding the ear with your finger and thumb for safety. 1

- The hair is fairly short on the top of the head from behind the eye to the back of the skull, and this is done with scissors. **1**

- Comb the beard forward and scissor downwards to give a deep-pointed look from the side view.

- The neck hair and body hair are shortened with scissors to about 2 to 4 inches (5 to 10 cm) and slightly tapered to the groin area. The underchest is fringed, and curves upwards towards the groin, giving the appearance of a deep chest. **2**

- The front of the chest is accentuated in shape from the base of the neck to the front leg. **2**

- The tail is fairly shortened with scissors and the undertail anal area is cut short. **2**

- The front legs are scissored to tidy, and the hair on the foot is cut round to shape it into a neat finish. Unlike the Poodle (page 270), the legs are not "indented" to show the feet; with the Black Russian, the feet appear as a continuation of the leg. **2**

- The back leg is trimmed to shape from the rump to the hock to accentuate angulations, and then from the hock to the foot. **2**

- The front part of the back leg has more hair

2

to accentuate the bend of the stifle, and then is trimmed down to the foot.

- The foot is cut in a round puff (i.e., a ball of hair) rather than a close cut.

- Trim under the foot to remove hair that might bunch and mat and cause the dog pain when it walks. Alternatively, clip this out with an Oster No. 15, ensuring that the top foot hair is left intact.

- Check the dog's nails, teeth and ears. Any hair inside the ears should be pulled out, as terriers should have an open ear canal.

- Note: the Black Russian Terrier needs trimming on a regular monthly basis (or for every show), much the same as the Kerry Blue (page 265).

BOUVIER DES FLANDRES

COAT: The coat is so abundant and thick that, when separated by hand, the skin is barely visible. Neither woolly nor curly, the hair should be about $2\frac{1}{2}$ inches (6 cm), gradually becoming shorter on the legs. The undercoat is dense and close-grained. On the crown of the head, the hair is short and is close on the ears. The eyebrows do not veil the eyes. The eyebrows, beard and mustache are accentuated to give a formidable appearance, but the eyes should be seen.

MAINTENANCE: The breed has a rough, dry coat that should be easy to maintain. A visit to the salon every eight weeks will keep the coat in hand – it should not be allowed to get out of control.

PROCEDURE

Equipment needed: Slicker brush, wide-toothed comb, scissors, clippers.

Breed tip: Grooming with a bristle brush encourages growth of the undercoat in this breed.

• Brush the entire coat with a slicker brush. This hair is best groomed in sections. Lift the layer of hair and brush from the parting downward. Untangler or coat protector will aid brushing and help to remove mats and unwanted dead hair, without unduly softening the coat.

• Be systematic. Start on the left back leg and work through the front and head. Turn the dog and work through the right side from the back leg.

• Comb through. However, if the hair is too dirty, it will cause unnecessary discomfort to the dog.

• The crown, or top of the head from just above the eyebrow to the occiput, is clipped with an Oster No. 10 or scissored down to shorten the appearance. This can also be done with your finger and thumb or a coarse stripping knife. Clipping is more common and the breeder will usually put in the triangular shape required on the crown before the puppy leaves them.

• The ears are clipped short and the edges are tidied with scissors. Take care to hold the ear to prevent nipping the skin.

• Comb through and either leave natural or thin/strip the sides of the cheeks to enhance the appearance.

• Thinners are used to taper the throat and chest hair toward the shoulder, or the hair can be cut shorter with scissors.

• The hair on the body is shortened with scissors to a length of about 2 inches (5 cm), and the legs are blended in level with the body hair and shortened to enhance their shape.

• Bathe with a protein shampoo and apply conditioner. Use a dematting balsam conditioner and brush it through the coat to help aid grooming, if required. Use a spray conditioner otherwise.

• Use absorbent towels, or some of the excess water can be blown from the coat using a power dryer.

- Finish with a blow-dry, using a pin brush to lift the coat and remove any remaining dead hair.

- Comb through with a wide-toothed comb. The coat may need a few days to settle before the dog is shown in the ring.

- Check the dog's nails, ears and teeth.

- When using thinning scissors, keep the tool pointing downwards with the fall of the coat – never cut crossways. Scissor the hair to enhance the deep chest. The dog should not appear cylindrical, and has very little tuck-up.

- Remove the hair from around the anal area with scissors or a No. 5 clipper blade.

- Also remove the hair between the pads underneath the foot, using a closer blade or scissors.

- Trim the foot around the circumference to give an appearance of a cat's paw.

- With the pet dog, the entire body is frequently cut shorter with scissors or clippers than on the show dog. Some owners request that this breed is clipped all over, leaving just a shortened beard, as with the terrier trim. To do this, use a No. 5 Oster, going with the growth before the bath, and tidy with a blade or scissors after blow-drying.

BRITTANY

COAT: The coat is dense, fine, rather flat and slightly wavy. The color is orange/white, liver/white, black/white, tricolor, roan or any of these colors.

MAINTENANCE: Not difficult to manage.

PROCEDURE

Equipment needed: Bristle brush or pin brush, fine-toothed comb.

Breed tip: Stripping may be required, but should never be noticeable – the breed should look as natural as possible.

- Brush the entire coat with a bristle or pin brush, using a slicker on the long parts and on the feathering.

- Comb through, removing dead hair with a molting comb. Use thinning shears where any thick hair may need a cleaner appearance.

- Bathe the coat in a protein shampoo and condition with a conditioning enhancer.

- Towel-dry and then air-, cage- or lightly blow-dry, going with the growth of the coat to achieve a flat finish.

• Check the Brittany's nails, ears and teeth.

• Use a stripping knife to remove untidy hairs from the head. Thinners can be used on the hair below the ears to give a smoother appearance. ▽

• Continue stripping using the knife or thinners, down with the growth of the hair to smooth and taper the entire body coat. Some groomers may find carding useful to smooth hairs on the body. (Hold a No. 15 Oster blade or a blunt stripping knife in your hand and strip it through the coat, as detailed.) Removal of the coat should never be noticeable. ▽

• Then, thin the coat where feathering is too profuse. Spray the coat with an enhancer or a protein coat

conditioner, giving a final brush to add luster and sheen, and to give a more flattened appearance.

• Interestingly, in the U.K., clippers should not be used on the Brittany, but thinning scissors are very useful for tidying the ears, neck and excess feathering on the legs. ▽

CESKY TERRIER

COAT: The coat is silky in texture, slightly wavy and has a metallic sheen. The color is gray (of any shade), occasionally with tan markings on the cheeks, the underside of the muzzle, the lower parts of the legs and under the tail. Small white patches and a white collar or tail tip are permissible. Very, very rarely, a brown specimen is found.

MAINTENANCE: The coat requires daily grooming and regular trimming. The legs and belly are left unclipped to form a low skirt, while the hair on the foreface is grown into a beard and eyebrows. The hair on the body should be no more than ½ inch (1.5 cm) long.

PROCEDURE

Equipment needed: Slicker brush, wide-toothed comb, thinning and straight scissors, and clippers with No. 10 and No. 7F blades.

Breed tip: A slicker brush should never be used on a show dog's coat, which should be brushed with a bristle brush instead. Pet dogs should be trimmed approximately every eight weeks.

• Brush through the long hair with a slicker to remove tangles, paying attention to under the arm where mats may form.

• Bathe the dog using a combined shampoo/conditioner and make sure you rinse thoroughly.

• Blow-dry the coat, combing through the long hair with a wide-toothed comb.

• Clip the skull with an Oster No. 7F, from above the eyes moving back to the neck. Clip the ears against the growth of the hair, using a No. 10.

• Carefully trim the edges of the ears with scissors.

• Using a No. 7F and clipping against the growth of the hair, clip from 1 inch (2.5 cm) below the point of the elbow, over the shoulder and up the neck. Follow a horizontal line between the legs to the throat and up to a line from the edge of the mouth via the corner of the eye to the top edge of the ear.

• Clip the neck and body with a No. 7F, leaving a skirt.

• Using a No. 7F and clipping against the direction of hair growth, clip the hindquarters from just above the hock to the groin. Leave the feathering on the front of the hindlegs, as well as the hair from the hock to the foot.

• Clip the tail from base to the tip and around the anus area.

• Blend the different lengths of hair using thinning shears.

• Comb through with a wide-toothed comb.

• Trim under the feet and between the pads to prevent the hair from forming mats.

• Thin the beard and leg hair with thinning shears as necessary. Trim around the feet and the ends of the skirt. The finish should look natural, with no hard edges.

• Check the dog's nails, ears and teeth.

feathering around their stifles shaped. Cutting to shape is not recommended, as plucking is relatively easy and looks more natural. The feathering should reach just to the knuckle, but it should be tapered, and not left looking like plus-fours! Shape down the hock to the pad. Do not trim the hocks too closely, as this makes for a spindly look.

• The tail should be thick at the root, tapering to a fine tip. Comb the feathering thoroughly and pluck out unwanted hair. The tail feathering should be as thick as the feathering on the legs – the aim is to achieve a balance throughout the whole coat. Plucking out the excess hair on the tail should create a neat, smooth finish on the top side of the tail and nicely but not overly thick feathering underneath. Trim the tail and cut neatly underneath it, shaping the feathering down to the top of the hock.

• Bathe the Cocker in a suitable shampoo and apply conditioner to help enhance the coat's appearance and to encourage it to lie flat.

• Blow the coat dry while brushing (with a pin brush) in the direction of the hair growth.

• Check the dog's nails, ears and teeth.

• Trim the clean hair from the hock down to the foot.

• Trim the toes to a round appearance, and take out any surplus hair from between the pads under the foot. Excess, untidy hair should be plucked out, but do not remove too much as this can look very ugly, and is not desirable in the show ring. Aim to achieve a neat and even, close-cut finish. In pet dogs, the hair between the toes is often extremely matted and dirty. This can lead to skin problems, so it is advisable for the pet owner to remove whatever hair has not been thoroughly cleaned by bathing.

• Comb through the feathering.

• When finished, the coat should look clean, and is stripped, thinned, carded or clipped with the hair growth, depending on the coat texture and whether the dog is a show specimen or a pet. This process can be helped by polishing the coat with a soft chamois cloth, which should leave it gleaming with good health and condition.

ENGLISH SPRINGER SPANIEL

COAT: The coat is close, straight and weather-resistant, never coarse. The feathering on the ears, forelegs, body and hindquarters is moderate. However, some ears seem to grow profusely and are better trimmed shorter to avoid matting and the collection of debris.

MAINTENANCE: Regular attention to the coat is necessary, which may include stripping, thinning and, sadly, even clipping – in the case of some pet dogs that have "runaway" coats. However, the natural look is desired and less trimming rather than more is usually sufficient to keep this breed looking good.

PROCEDURE

Equipment needed: Pin brush or slicker, metal comb.

Breed tip: Household rubber gloves or rubber thimbles will make the removal of dead, wispy hairs much easier – particularly on the top of the head and on the body coat.

- Brush the body and feathering with a pin brush or slicker, removing tangles with a metal comb.

- For a pet groom, trim (with thinning scissors) all the hair immediately under the ear. This will allow the air to pass freely into the ear and help prevent infection. Clean regularly with a proprietary ear cleaner.

- Carding is useful to thin the body hair where required. Use thinning shears where excess hair falls to give a tidy, clean – but not overtrimmed – look.

- Bathe the dog in a suitable shampoo.

- Lightly blow-dry the coat, going in the direction of the growth of the hair to dry it flat, or cage-dry after combing through the coat when wet.

- Check the dog's nails, ears and teeth.

- Check underneath the feet for the presence of debris and unwanted hair.

- Trim any excess hair from the back of the hocks to neaten, giving a clean look.

- Tidy the feet to a well-rounded, tight appearance.

- For a show trim, trim the hair underneath the ears so they lie flat.

- Using trimming scissors, trim the hair on the ears to about one-third of the way down, to achieve a smooth finish. **1**

- Next, pluck out long hairs from the top of the dog's head. **1**

- Trim the hair under the chin and on the brisket bone, again using thinning scissors. Thin the hair on the shoulders and blend the hair into the body. 1

- Dead hair on the flanks and from the occiput and down the neck and back should be plucked out using finger and thumb. Scissors should not be used. 1

- The hair around the tail should be trimmed to a neat appearance, and hair around the anus should be removed. Blend in to surrounding hair by using thinning scissors. 1

- Trim the hair around each foot to neaten the shape, and cut any excess hair in between the toes and underneath the foot.

- Use thinning scissors to trim the hair and graduate back to the "stopper pad" to blend the hair in.

- Remove hair from the hocks, trimming to a close, smooth finish. Again, use thinning scissors.

FIELD SPANIEL

COAT: The coat is long, flat, glossy and silky in texture. It is never curly or wiry, but rather dense and weatherproof. Abundant feathering is seen on the chest, under the body and behind the legs, but the line is clean from the hock to the ground.

The color is black, liver or roan, or any of these with tan markings.

MAINTENANCE: Relatively easy to look after, the Field Spaniel needs regular brushing and combing, and stripping or thinning.

Equipment needed: Bristle brush, medium-toothed comb, thinning scissors, stripping knife, scissors.

Breed tip: The Field Spaniel coat should be as flat as possible.

- Brush with a bristle brush to remove dead hairs and tangles that may have formed in the feathering, under the arms and particularly around the ears.

- After brushing, thoroughly comb through with a medium-toothed comb.

- Using thinning shears or your finger and thumb, remove thick hair on the head to give a neat, clean appearance.

- Body hair is stripped or thinned where necessary to give a flat look.

- Bathe the dog in a suitable shampoo and conditioner to help enhance the gleam of the coat.

- Lightly blow-dry in the direction of the hair growth.

- Check the Field Spaniel's nails, ears and teeth.

- Comb through once more, and remove stray hairs with your finger and thumb. Alternatively, use thinning shears to produce a flat appearance.

- For pet dogs, lightly spray with a coat finish if extra shine is required. (Show dogs shouldn't have anything applied to the coat.)

KERRY BLUE TERRIER

COAT: The coat is quite a feature of this breed, being thick, soft and silky, and it does not shed. The coat, as well as being soft and silky, is plentiful and wavy. Puppies are born black and can take up to 18 months to clear to blue, of which there are many shades.

MAINTENANCE: It needs considerable trimming to keep it looking smart.

PROCEDURE

Equipment needed: Slicker brush, wide-toothed comb, scissors or clippers.

Breed tip: Preparing for the show ring, the Kerry Blue is washed and left to dry in warm air. The dog is then brushed, combed and scissored all over.

The pet Kerry is more often clipped, rather than scissored, to save time and money. A coarse blade should be used for this, with a finer one on the head.

- Brush the entire coat, including the beard, with a slicker.

- Comb through with a wide- or medium-toothed comb to remove all tangles.

- Bathe in a suitable shampoo for the blue coat, and then apply conditioner. Use a purifying shampoo and conditioning mask when required, up to three times a year.

- Dry in a cage or in warm air.

- Check the dog's nails, ears and teeth.

- The head is clipped. Using a No. 10 blade, clip the head – working away from the eye and leaving the eyebrows intact, clip or scissor back across the skull, leaving hair from the top eye level to form the shape of the face (see below). Make sure you work with the direction of the hair growth. 1 2

- Next clip the ears, preferably using a slightly smaller blade. Going against the hair growth will produce shorter results. Neaten the edges with scissors. 1 2

- Clip from the outer corner of the eye, backwards to the point of the neck. Trim down from this same marker to the edge of the mouth and under the chin to where you can feel a definite lump under the chin. Clip down the throat to taper at the base of the neck or the Adam's apple to a V-shape.

- Clip the body with the Oster No. 7/5/4, depending on the length required. Alternatively, scissor with the growth of the hair to the shoulders, down and back across the rib cage, down the back to the tail, and up the tail. Clip the body to leave a rise over the hip joint or the bone where the back leg begins 1. All the leg hair is neatly blended into the shorter body hair.

- Clip under the tail upward, and then down the anal area. 3

- Blend in the legs with scissors to complement the dog's angulations, giving shape.

- The front legs are blended in from the elbow down, to incorporate the feet. 2

- Scissor the hair out from underneath each foot.

- Trim the edge of the ears to neaten their appearance.

- Comb the Kerry Blue's eyebrows and beard forward. Next, trim the eyebrows and beard with the scissors pointing forward toward the nose. The hair between the eyes is shaped in a graduated fashion, so that face hair is prevented from falling sideways and impairing the dog's vision, particularly when on the move. 1 2

- Spray lightly with a coat gloss conditioner, if required.

- The hair on the head is taken shorter with clippers or scissors. With the show dog, the coat is scissored throughout as previously stated.

- Note: show dogs are clipped on the head as for pets, although many owners prefer scissoring, and it is always a good idea to check first with the breed standard recommendation.

LÖWCHEN

COAT: It has a fine, long, single coat, which comes in any color, marking or combination of both. The Löwchen cannot be bred for color – you get what you get!

MAINTENANCE: Its body is clipped from the last rib, down over the rear and down the back leg to the hock. It is clipped down the tail to leave one-third of the tail as plumage. It is also clipped from the elbow to just above the wrist.

The Löwchen requires regular brushing and grooming – this is a breed whose coat can mat within 20 minutes of bathing!

PROCEDURE

Equipment needed: Exhibitors tend to use a combination of clippers and a wide-toothed comb, although pet owners can manage the coat using a pin brush and a comb.

Breed tip: The soft coat will mat if not regularly brushed.

- Comb through with a wide-toothed comb or a pin brush.

- Bathe in a good-quality dog shampoo. Rinse well.

- Apply conditioning cream.

- Dry with a blower while gently brushing the hair with a pin brush or wide-toothed comb.

- If clipping your dog (most pet owners will not bother), use your chosen blade size. This is a matter of personal choice – some people use a No. 5 blade, while others use a No. 30 blade. Popular choices are No. 10 and No. 15 blades, which clip quite close to the body. Start just behind the last rib and incorporate the whole back leg down to the hock. 1

- Clip the front leg with your chosen blade size. Clip from just below the elbow to a line that is level with the start of the hair left at the hock on the back leg. 1

- Clip two-thirds of the tail with your blade from the base up, leaving a plumage on the end. 1

- Comb all plumage.

- Check the dog's nails, ears and teeth.

PORTUGUESE WATER DOG

▲ *The "Retriever" trim*

268

COAT: The coat is described as profuse. There are two distinct types, born without undercoats: (a) Hair fairly long and loosely waved with a slight sheen; hair on head erect, ears well feathered; (b) Hair short, fairly harsh and dense, compact curls, lacking luster, head hair similar to body, hair on ears somewhat wavy.

MAINTENANCE: The hair doesn't molt, and needs brushing and combing frequently. These dogs are traditionally clipped on the face, hindquarters and on part of the tail, leaving a profuse plume at the end. The front end of the dog's coat is left to grow naturally.

PROCEDURE

Equipment needed: Slicker/pin brush, wide-toothed comb, clippers.

Breed tip: The pet dog can be clipped to about $\frac{1}{2}$ inch (1.25 cm) all over – this is called the "Retriever" trim (see page 268) and is used for showing in the U.S.

- Brush through the coat, removing tangles.

- Using an Oster No. 10 or 15 blade, clip the face from the corner of the eye to the corner of the ear in straight line.

- Clip down the muzzle from the eye.

- Clip the neck to the point of the throat.

- Clip the abdomen area.

- Clip the complete back leg from the last rib, including the back toes, with an Oster No. 10 or 15. Clip the tail two-thirds from the base to leave plumage on the remaining third.

- Clip the hair from between the pads underneath the feet.

- Bathe the dog in a suitable shampoo and apply a conditioner.

- Blow the hair dry using a pin brush, then comb with a wide-toothed comb.

- Remember to check the dog's nails, ears and teeth.

269

17 THE POODLE

CORDED POODLE

For details on coat care for the Corded Poodle, see page 75 (Chapter 10).

Featured: the Standard Poodle in "Lamb" trim is Tragapanz Chelsea Girl, owned by Carol Flatt.

COAT: The Poodle is the most intriguing of all breeds to trim – there are just so many styles into which its unique nonmolting coat can be artistically contoured.

MAINTENANCE: Poodle coats need constant attention. Pet owners invariably forget to brush their dogs, and they come into the grooming salon every six weeks or so with mats and tangles in their coats.

Once upon a time, the only considerate and kind way to deal with such felted mats was to get underneath the mat with a fine blade and clip it off.

With today's many preparations, conditioners and mat-breakers, the groomer has a wider choice and more capacity to sort out a neglected coat.

However, the prime consideration must be the welfare of the dog, and if the best solution is to clip off the coat, then this must be done. Given time, the coat will grow again.

POODLE EARS

Poodle ears have hair growing inside them. It is part of the grooming procedure to deal with this, and an experienced groomer should show a novice how to do this painlessly. You should lift the flap of the ear against the head, thereby protecting the inner ear. Hold the muzzle to keep the dog still, and then use forceps to tease out tiny bits of hair at a time. It is always a good idea to use some ear powder first, as this will help loosen the hair.

Where brown wax is evident, mites have probably invaded, so clean the ear with alcohol or ear cleaner and apply ear powder before and after removing as much of the offending mess as possible. Lemon juice and witch hazel ear-cleaning preparations are also available for this. This procedure may need to be repeated daily until the problem has cleared up.

SCISSOR WORK

There is a lot of scissor work to be done on a Poodle and only practice will allow the groomer to achieve a smooth, almost satin finish to the well-cared-for coat. Finishing is an art that some excel at more than others.

Different scissors give different finishes and the groomer must try several pairs of scissors in order to find the pair right for them. Most sales outlets are happy to help you choose the right type. Scissors vary in price, and to sustain the outstanding presentation that some groomers achieve it is imperative to buy high-quality equipment, such as clippers, scissors, shampoo and finishing sculpture conditioner. It really does make a difference and the investment is worthwhile.

Finishing is achieved by literally skimming over the coat with the scissors accurately placed to edge the coat. As the Poodle coat grows and moves constantly, and it has a natural tendency to curl despite straightening conditioners, this finish will not last, but still the dog will look expertly smart.

Good scissoring is an art. It is fascinating to watch groomers from different parts of the world scissoring in their own style to achieve perfection. If you visit grooming seminars, you will be able to see this interesting skill in action, and all the groomers' different styles. Some fluff the hair outwards and let it fall before commencing scissoring, while some comb it upwards. Some will say one way is the only correct way, but I have seen dogs turned out to sheer perfection both ways.

The same applies to how you hold a pair of scissors. Some use thumb and index, some thumb and middle finger, while others use thumb and fourth finger. I try all ways, and I don't see any difference! However, I do like scissors with a guard.

PROCEDURE

With all styles, the Poodle will need to have its feet, face and tail clipped. We will deal with this first. There are certain rules to observe:

- Apart from the feet, it is always safer to use clippers with the growth of coat to prevent rashing or grazing the skin.

- Where the face is concerned, always clip away from the eye.

- Unless you are experienced using clippers, it is quite likely that you will need time to get around all the delicate clipped parts of the Poodle, so use clipper lubricant frequently, every 10 minutes or less, and check the blade of the clipper for heat by putting it on your face. As soon as it feels more than a little warm, change the blade. Dogs have been burned with hot blades and it takes a long time for them to regain their confidence. My personal preference is for Aesculap blades.

FEET

Use blades that are meant for a closer finish on the dark colors only. Some people boast that they use a No. 40 blade on the feet and face, but the dogs invariably look as though they are grazed the next day, and I don't see why anyone wants to skin a Poodle. I have judged them in the show ring when their faces are livid red and even bleeding, and I consider this very wrong indeed. Feet can take a closer blade with less ill effect.

- Starting at the rear right foot (being sure the dog is standing square and is comfortable), hold the leg just beneath the hock joint, just above the foot. Take care that the foot is underneath the dog and not pulled out to the side. ▼

- Gently press open the toes with your fingers and clip the hair away from around the nails, flexing your wrist to turn the clipper to achieve this, and not twisting the dog's foot.

271

• Clip up each toe in turn, taking the hair from between the toes and being careful to avoid ramming the clipper into the web. Make sure you clip to the base of the toe and no higher, otherwise you will spoil the finished

appearance and give the Poodle what is known as a "chicken look."

• Clip each foot in turn. Remember to change the blade if it gets too warm.

▼ 1

▼ 2

FACE

For the Poodle's face, we use an Oster No. 10 blade for most pet dogs and, for the thicker coat, a No. 15. The show dog is usually clipped closer with a No. 30, but this is not always advisable with a cream or white face. Always keep the blade as flat as possible without putting undue pressure on the skin.

• Hold the dog's muzzle in the right hand, folding the ear back over the head, and clip from the corner of the eye to the upper corner of the ear in a straight, neat line. ▼

• Clip under the eye to the inner corner, then from between the eyes (at the stop) down to the tip of the nose. ▼ ▼

▼ 1

- Clip from under the eye toward the muzzle to the nose. Repeat on other side of the face. ▼2 ▼4

- From the base of the ear, clip down to the point of the throat – the Adam's apple. ▼3 ▼4

- Clip the chin from the edge of the mouth to the nose, taking care to tighten the loose skin at all times. ▼4

- For the show Poodle, the neck is clipped into a U-shape, which involves shaving the hair down to an inch or two above the breastbone, depending on the style of the mane, and the emphasis required to show off the length of the neck. ▼3 ▼4

- Note: if you are unsure of the thickness of the facial hair, first clip the face with the coarser No. 10 blade – you can always take more off later, but if you start with, say, a No. 30 and it is too close for that individual dog, you could be in trouble, causing clipper rash, grazing or worse.

▼2

TAIL

Use a No. 15 Oster.

* Clip one-third of the (usually docked) tail from the base, leaving enough hair to create a pompom. 1

* Clip under the tail with a No. 10 blade, being careful not to use a clipper on the bulge of the anus. 2

BODY

"LAMB" CLIP

Use a No. 5 (summer) or a No. 4 (winter) Oster (for a longer finish).

* Clip from the base of the dog's head, just beneath the ears, down the top and underneath the neck, following the direction of hair growth. 1

* Lift the leg and clip under the arm and along the chest to the groin. 2 3 4

* Clip the neck to just above shoulder level, down the back to the tail, and just above the hip. Then clip along and downward over the rib cage to the groin. 3 5

* Clip underneath the body – the stomach and

the groin – carefully taking hair from around the genitals. Always hold the delicate parts as you groom, to ensure safety. ▽3 ▽4

• Brush through the remaining hair, trousers, topknot and tail, removing all tangles with a slicker brush and a wide-toothed comb. Where necessary, to prevent causing the dog too much discomfort, use a mat-breaker. Anti-tangle conditioner can help too. ▽6

• Bathe the Poodle in a suitable natural, enhancing shampoo (such as tea tree and lavender), or a protein coat-strengthening formula with consideration to color and condition of the coat. ▽7

• Use a quality conditioner, such as sculpture finish, to aid scissoring.

• Blow the coat dry, brushing all the time in sections from the bottom of the leg upward with a pin brush or slicker. ▽8

• Check the dog's nails ▽9, ears ▽10 and teeth ▽11.

• Tidy all clipped areas where required by going over these parts with the same depth of blade as before.

• Hem the leg hair by neatening and blending the edge of the hair at the bottom of the leg, just above the toes. ▽12

• Scissor the legs, going with the contours of the body, or by using a silhouette line ▽3 ▽13. To do this contour edge, or to snip the hair, hold the scissors at a slight angle, pointing upward, and continue the line from bottom to top. Then take the next line and blend into the first line. Do not cut crossways (apart from when hemming across the toes). Trim with the scissors pointing downward or upward, at a slight angle but never crossways (apart from when hemming). Finally, skim across the hair to blend in any

stray hairs. Note: some groomers work (scissor) down from the body to the foot – it makes no difference if they get the correct neat finish.

• Holding the dog's muzzle, comb the head hair forward and scissor a topknot across the eye upward. ▽14

• Comb the hair to the left and trim across the top of the ears and the back of the neck, then repeat on the right side. ▽15

• Trim over the top, taking care to leave a nice topknot, but be sure that the dog can see clearly. ▽16

• For the tail, hold the pompom in one hand at the end of the dock (further up if the dock is short). Then cut straight across ▽17. Allow the hair to fall, and comb outwards. Hold up the tail at the tip and comb the hair outward, then scissor to a round appearance ▽18 or, in the case of a long tail, it may be more effective to trim into a brush, rather like that of a retriever.

• The finished dog. ▽19

▽1

2

3

4

5

6

7

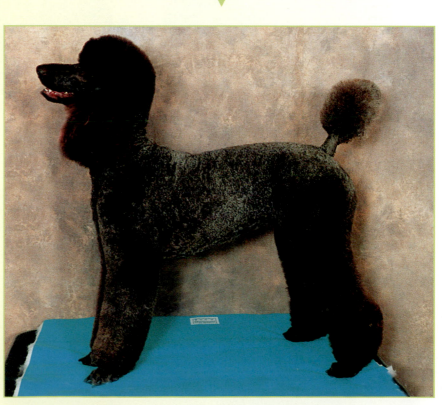

"SPORTING" OR "UTILITY" CLIP

Use a No. 5 Oster for the summer clip and a No. 4 for the winter clip. A thick coat can happily be taken down with the No. 10, going with the growth of the hair, in the summertime.

- Clip the neck from the base of the head, down over the shoulder, down the back to the tail, down and along the rib cage and under the chest, stomach and groin area. 1

- Clip the back leg, inside and out, to an inch above the hock joint. Then, with an eyeline to balance, clip inside and out of the front leg to the same level. For the eyeline, just look at where the clip mark of the back leg ends and draw an imaginary line across to the front leg. 1

- Bathe and dry the Poodle, as for the "Lamb" clip (page 274).

- Check the nails, ears and teeth.

- Scissor the topknot as for the "Lamb" clip (page 274).

- Comb the long hair on the legs outward (bracelets) and scissor the bracelets into an oval shape.

- Trim the dog's tail as you would for the "Lamb" clip (page 274).

"DUTCH" CLIP

Use a No. 10 Oster.

- Clip the face, feet and tail, as with the instructions for the previous trims.

- Clip under the neck to the point of the breastbone, and then clip the rest of the neck to about 2 inches (5 cm) just above the withers. 1

- Taking a direct line, shave a blade's width between the shoulders, across the withers, and continue the line to the base of tail. 1

- Clip the abdomen from the groin to the navel and then downward, incorporating the insides of the thighs. 1

- Brush through the remaining unclipped hair with a slicker, and comb out any tangles.

- Bathe the dog in a suitable shampoo as for the "Lamb" clip (page 274).

- Blow-dry the coat, as described for the "Lamb" clip (see page 274).

- Check the dog's nails, ears and teeth.

- Go over the clipped part of the body to ensure a tidy finish.

- Scissor the topknot and tail as for the "Lamb" clip (page 274).

- Scissor the back legs to a neat finish, leaving a pronounced curve at the edge of the clipped parts, to give the impression that it is standing off. 1

- Scissor the front legs, leaving a pronounced curve to give the impression of the hair standing off the body. Scissor the front, leaving another pronounced curve that stands off from the body, rather than being blended into it. 1

1

"FULL PUPPY" CLIP

A lot of time and effort goes into maintaining this style. It is mostly seen on puppies exhibited in the U.S. show ring, although there are some pet owners who adore their Poodles in this stunning trim and are happy to pay for the time and expertise the groomer takes in turning out an evenly scissored finish.

- Clip the face, feet and tail, as with the previous instruction.

- Thoroughly groom the coat with a slicker or pin brush, followed by a wide-toothed comb.

- Clip under the stomach/abdomen from the groin to the navel with a No. 10 blade. **1**

- Bathe the dog in a suitable shampoo for the color and condition of the coat and apply a quality conditioner to aid scissor work.

- Blow-dry the hair away from the body, lifting with a pin brush to ensure it does not curl.

- Trim around the bottom of the legs to allow a peep at the toes. **1**

- Snip off the very fine ends of hair to an even and dense-looking finish. As the coat grows in length, scissor slightly shorter at the base of the tail, blending the hair up toward the body to obtain an effective, pleasing, glamorous shape. **1**

- Scissor the dog's tail as you would for the "Lamb" clip (see page 274).

"PUPPY LION" (OR "T-CLIP")

Strictly, the "Puppy Lion" and "T-clips" are different – the Scandinavian version of the "Puppy" clip accentuates the outlines slightly more.

In Britain, this trim is seen frequently in the show ring. In the U.S., show Poodles must be clipped into the traditional "Lion" at the age of 12 months.

- Clip the feet, face and tail, and groom and bathe the dog as for the "Puppy" clip (see page 281).

- Clip the abdomen area.

- Feel the body to ascertain the location of the last rib. For the uninitiated, it is a good idea to put a narrow bandage around the dog at just below this point to distinguish an even line and to be sure the balance is right. (Roughly one-third is trimmed shorter while two-thirds is left for the mane.)

- With the scissors held straight, cut upward along the edge of your line or bandage, from the near side, up one side, over the body and down the other side. This is more easily

achieved when the dog is standing square with its rear end toward you. Remove your "guideline" bandage.

- In the "Puppy Lion"/"T-clip" (called "pajamas" by some) the back legs are trimmed with scissors as with the "Lamb" clip, but are left longer from the stifle down, and shaped over the hock with more accent on the rear angulations (to show, or to make the leg appear more angulated than it might be – clever trimming often scores more goals).

- Once you are well practiced with scissors, and if you have a good eye for the artwork involved, you can use a picture of your favorite dog and copy the up-to-the-minute trimming or the fashion of the current time.

- Flick the mane with the comb and allow the dog to shake and the hair to settle. Then, keeping the scissors level, scissor around, rather like skimming over the coat. The aim is to achieve a blend where the mane meets the shorter back hair to enhance the appearance of a well-defined neck.

- Work around the mane, shaping the incline from the brisket up toward the ear.

- Scissor the front legs to a tubular shape, accentuating where they join the mane at the elbow with a slight indent.

- Scissor the tail like the "Lamb" clip (page 274).

"TRADITIONAL LION" ("FULL PACK" OR "ENGLISH SADDLE")

- Clip the feet, face and tail.

- Groom, bathe, condition and blow the hair dry as for the "Puppy" clip (page 281).

- Part the coat behind the rib cage as in the "Puppy Lion" (page 282). It is always advisable to clip the mane in before the back end to make it easier to achieve a good balance. Again, a bandage can be used for forming lines. This is always a good idea as you can tie it around at the given points and move it up or down to achieve a balance before putting your scissors in. Once you've snipped, there is no turning back!

- Apply the bandage about 2 inches (5 cm) above the wrist, and look to see if this will allow you to scissor a nice oval bracelet. Cut above the bandage line, clip with a No. 10 up the front leg to remove the hair up to the joint of the elbow. Do not clip over the elbow. Trim the bracelet by combing the hair outward and allowing it to fall naturally. Then scissor the ends, tipping (scissoring) to form an oval shape. ▮

- Scissor around the bottom of the mane to achieve a ball finish. ▮

- Feel for the hock joint and apply the bandage about 1 inch (2.5 cm) above. ▮

- Feel for the stifle joint, and apply a second bandage to define. Stand back and check that there is a good balance between the three defined points. Move the bandage slightly up or down until you feel happy that the dog looks right. ▮

- With the scissors, cut a thin line above the bandage. These points can be carefully clipped, or defined with scissors.

- When starting on the other leg, do check that your lines correspond from behind (as seen in the illustration), otherwise the trim will look odd and unbalanced. Remember, once the scissors have cut, there is no turning back.

- Comb the individual three sections of hair on the back leg upward and outward, and then allow it to fall or settle naturally. Scissor each section to a smooth, rounded finish.

- Scissor the tail as for the "Lamb" clip (see page 274).

"CONTINENTAL LION" CLIP

Most of the Poodles that are shown in the United States are put into this clip at 12 months of age. It takes less time than the "Traditional" or "Puppy" clips, but still there is a lot of work here.

• Clip the feet, face and tail, and bathe, condition and blow the hair dry as for the "Puppy" clip (page 281).

• Cut in the front end (mane) as for the "Lion" (page 283), including scissoring to finish.

• For beginners, it is a good idea to place a saucer on the hip joint to define a rosette. Take the scissors and cut around the saucer. Remove the saucer and you will reveal a large rosette. Depending on whether the dog is longer than it should be in the back, or perfectly proportioned, the saucer can be moved backward or forward to achieve the best balance before cutting commences.

• With a No. 10 blade, start clipping from a position just above the hock joint and clip up to your newly made rosette. Clip around this, being careful not to clip the rosette itself. Clip the narrow area between the end of the mane and the rosette. **1**

• Lifting the hair with a comb, scissor around the rosette to achieve a smart, round puff of hair. **1**

• Trim the tail as for the "Puppy" clip (page 281).

1

INDEX OF BREEDS

D

E

F

G

H

I

J

K

L

M

N

O